'A Chance in a Million?'

Scottish Avalanches

R. D. Barton   D. S. B. Wright

with illustrations drawn by D. Evans

The Scottish Mountaineering Trust

First published in Great Britain in 1985 by
The Scottish Mountaineering Trust

Distributed by Cordee
3a De Montfort Street,
Leicester LE1 7HD

Barton, Bob
   A chance in a million: Scottish avalanches
   for climbers and skiers.
   1. Avalanches—Scotland
   I. Title   II. Wright, Blyth
   551.57'848'09411   QC929.A8

   ISBN 0-907521-11-8

Filmset by Advanced Filmsetters (Glasgow) Ltd
Printed by Brown, Son & Ferguson, Glasgow
Bound by James Gowans, Glasgow

Contents

Preface

We hope that this book will be of value to those who climb or ski in the Scottish mountains and that it encourages an informed enjoyment of the delights of the winter hills.

We are indebted to our employers, the Scottish Sports Council, who have encouraged the production of this book and to Fred Harper who originally suggested the need for such a text and who has seen it through to completion.

André Roch originally stimulated our interest in the subject and Eric Langmuir both laid the foundations of a study of Scottish avalanches and made helpful suggestions towards the present book. Our colleagues at Glenmore Lodge were generous in sharing their experiences and tolerant of the problems of authorship, whilst a number of other people kindly provided eye-witness accounts of avalanche incidents.

Dudley Evans converted rough sketches into clear diagrams with great flair, and Penny Sandison, Susan Smith and Carolyne Lucas typed the manuscript. Finally, Peter Hodgkiss gave painstaking assistance in preparing and editing the book for the printer.

All these and others unmentioned deserve our heartfelt thanks but should be absolved from any responsibility for errors in the text for which we alone must be blamed.

R. D. Barton   D. S. B. Wright

Units of measurement

Metric units of distance are used in this book except in anecdotal accounts, where the original Imperial units have been retained. Windspeed is described in knots since this unit is still in meteorological use and is more easily related to practical experience than is metres per second (1 knot = 0·51 metres per second). Temperature is given in degrees Celsius (Centigrade).

1 A Short History

Avalanches in the Glens

Even the relatively populous Highland Glens of the pre-Clearances period seemed to have gone unscathed by avalanche. The recorded history of Scottish avalanche tells of no such major tragedies as are commonplace in the Alps. Indeed, no Scottish incident compares with the disaster which overtook the English village of Lewes in Sussex in 1836. On December 27 that year, a huge avalanche descended from the comparatively short slope above the village, destroying several cottages and killing eight of the inhabitants. Their communal grave remains to testify to the event, as does the name of a local inn, "*The Snowdrop*".

Few other examples exist in Scotland or England of catastrophic avalanches invading populated areas, although some accidents have happened to inhabitants of hill regions. Bridging the gap between the Lewes incident and the first mountaineering avalanches of the next century, an avalanche occurred on February 27, 1888, beneath Whinstone Lee Tor in Derbyshire. It was large enough to bury two brothers, Frank and Willie Walker of Riding House, Derwent. Frank had a foot protruding and was rescued alive after being found by dogs—Willie Walker was less fortunate and was dead when found, buried "yards deep" in the debris.

Scotland's first recorded fatal avalanche antedates the Lewes event by many years. Five men died in this, the notorious "*Loss of Gaick*", which remains today the only occasion when a Scottish avalanche has destroyed a human habitation, albeit a seasonal and remote one. The principal in this tragedy was John Macpherson, a retired Captain of the 82nd Regiment and at the time of the accident in 1800, the tenant of the farm of Ballachroan near Kingussie and of the Forest of Gaick. Macpherson enjoyed a certain unpopularity in the Badenoch area because of his previous exploits as a highly successful recruiting officer. Perhaps because of this, as well as his dark complexion, he was known as the *"Black Officer"* or *"an Othaichear Dubh"* and was popularly supposed to be in league with the Devil.

Whatever his affiliation, the Black Officer died in the opening days of the new century, about January 4, 1800, along with his hunting companions James Grant, Duncan Macfarlane, Donald Macgillivray and John Macpherson. They were overwhelmed, probably as they slept, in a small cottage near the site of the present Gaick Lodge. Friends, alarmed at their failure to return from the hunting trip, raised a search party. They found on the site of the cottage only a huge mound of snow. Digging revealed the shattered remnants of the building, its roof gone and its walls almost totally destroyed. Inside they found four bodies, including that of the Captain. One or perhaps two bodies lay on a rough wooden bed, the others on the ground along with the bodies of the dogs. Only the melting of the snow weeks later enabled the body of Donald Macfarlane to be found some distance from the cottage, "lying on his side with his right hand raised, pointing heavenwards."

A great body of myth and legend surrounds this event and local opinion was quick to assign supernatural significance to many aspects of the story. This makes interesting comparison with the similar attitudes of Alpine villagers towards avalanche disasters. They, too, commonly regarded such happenings as inevitable and unforeseeable, either as Acts of God or the work of evil spirits. Some climbers and skiers in Scotland apparently still adhere to this fatalistic philosophy!

The magnitude of the Gaick avalanche must have been altogether exceptional by Scottish standards. At least two accounts mention that debris was scattered to a distance of between four and five hundred metres. This would mean that the avalanche completely blocked the floor of the glen at that point. Large avalanches are not altogether uncommon in Scotland, but in the sparsely populated glens of modern times, few threaten the homes of men.

Isolated incidents occur, nonetheless. In February of 1946 an avalanche came down near the stalker's house at Moulzie above Glen Clova, falling about 350 m to sweep across the River South Esk on a front of about 150 m and piling up at the 300 m contour. Huge quantities of stones and turf were carried down and although this avalanche took no human victims, it is remembered locally for the large number of deer which it killed.

But it is to Gaick that we must return for the nearest miss and also to close the book which Gaick opened on nineteenth century avalanches. ... On Christmas Eve, 1899, a hundred years almost to the week after the famous disaster, the keeper and his family sat up late at the present Lodge, waiting to open their Christmas presents. A great noise was heard and inspection later revealed that a huge avalanche had swept down, crossing the site of the disaster of 1800 and stopping only some 30 or 40 m short of the new Lodge.

Another such avalanche is known to have occurred in the thirty years between 1885 and 1915: one of these destroyed the back wall of the old sheep fank immediately adjacent to the site of the Macpherson disaster. Future avalanche researchers might be amply repaid by spending their Christmas holiday at Gaick in 1999!

Despite incidents such as these, no substantial risk exists in Scotland to towns, villages, or communications, although it is not inconceivable that certain main roads could be threatened in exceptional conditions. The risk concerns rather those who use the mountains for recreation, winter hill walkers, snow and ice climbers, and off-piste skiers, who during the present century are almost the only avalanche victims in Scotland.

Accidents on the Mountains

Time spent in studying the misfortune of others is seldom wasted, which may perhaps explain the popularity of the pursuit. Thus, a study in detail of recorded avalanche accidents in this country may serve to dispel certain cherished illusions; at the same time, too much should not be read into the limited data available.

The basic problem facing the student of Scottish avalanche accidents lies in finding information giving an accurate picture of their incidence over the years. The writings of early Scottish climbing and skiing pioneers contain several references to avalanche incidents, some of a spectacular nature. Creag Meagaidh, Ben More, Cruach Ardrain and Ben Lui were known avalanche sites before official Mountain Rescue records began, although these incidents produced no serious injuries. However, the growing use of the hills in the thirties saw the first reports of accidents involving injury. In fact, most Scottish avalanche incidents have no serious consequences; an educated guess might be that one in every three or four incidents where hill-goers are avalanched actually results in an injury and/or Mountain Rescue call-out.

The following information is based on official published reports of Mountain Rescue incidents, the only more or less reliable source of accident information; allied to these are incidents known to the writers through their own observations and those of a wide circle of knowledgeable informants. It is, however, unlikely to be complete. Only accidents involving injury and/or Mountain Rescue call-out are noted.

The Figures

Overall Totals

The incidence of deaths and injuries due to avalanche is fairly random over the years, although the general trend is upwards.

Table 1. Avalanche accidents in Scotland

	Winters 1959–60 to 1968–69 inclusive	Winters 1969–70 to 1978–79 inclusive	Totals 1925 to end of winter 1979–80	Totals 1925 to end of winter 1982–83
Accidents	16	40	74	91
Persons involved (minimum)	43	97	195	244
Fatalities	4	16	26	30
Injured	20	57	108	126

Note: Only accidents involving injury or a Mountain Rescue call-out are noted.

However, in general and over ten-year periods, some factors are reasonably constant, i.e.,

an average of 2–3 persons is involved in each accident;
about one accident in three or four involves a fatality;
about two in every three persons involved is injured or killed.

The only real conclusion to be drawn here is that if a party is involved in an avalanche accident serious enough to warrant a call-out, the chance for each individual of death or injury is high.

Yearly Totals

It will easily be seen that since the early sixties, there has been a general trend upward in avalanche accidents, with several accidents reported in each of the last ten winters (1983) and fatalities in five of them.

Table 2. Graph of avalanche accidents in Scotland. Winters 1959–60 to 1982–83.

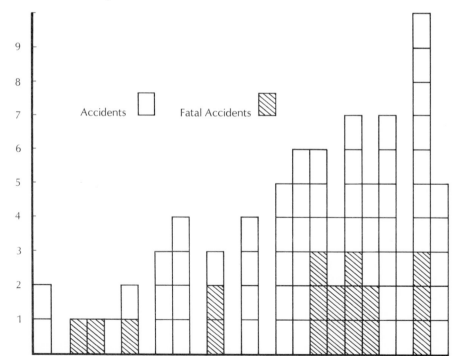

A Chance in a Million

Table 3. Avalanche accidents in Scotland. Frequency according to month. To end of winter 1982–83.

October	November	December	January	February	March	April
2	2	13	18	25	26	8

Recorded but undated accidents not listed.

According to Month of Year

Clearly, the high winter months of January, February and March produce most accidents, although the fact that December has seen more trouble than April is slightly surprising. It may be that a majority of climbers, particularly those from south of the Border, confine their activities to the peak season. Also, the wet snow avalanches which probably predominate in April, although potentially very destructive, are much more predictable than the typical early season wind-slab avalanche. It is interesting to note that, according to the records, cornice avalanches cause no more accidents in spring than during the rest of the winter. A cornice overloaded due to recent blizzard may be just as much of a hazzard as one weakened and overloaded due to thawing. Although only nine accidents due to cornice collapse are noted, it is sometimes difficult to differentiate them from the common case where the scarp underneath the cornice avalanches; also, several accidents recorded only as due to avalanche, must undoubtedly have been due to cornice collapse or to cornice-triggered avalanche.

Popular Misconceptions

Open Slopes

As long ago as 1961 Malcolm Smith, Editor of the SMC Cairngorms Area Climbers' Guide, warned "...the fact that open-slope avalanches are common in the area, despite the textbooks, ...is not generally appreciated." What is true for the Cairngorms applies equally to other mountain areas—at least 33 of the 95 avalanche accidents recorded in Scotland have been on open slopes rather than gullies. And still, many climbers and skiers seem unaware of the dangers. Even the innocent-looking snow apron below the cliffs in many winter climbing corries may produce dangerous avalanches. At least 11 such accidents are recorded. Open-slope avalanches can be of Alpine proportions, a few being recorded up to nearly a kilometre in width and with break-off walls of three to five metres.

Miraculously, some Scottish parties have survived avalanches of this magnitude, notably a party of eight descending from the Cairngorm plateau towards Coire an Lochain on March 10, 1965. See p. 94.

The largest Scottish avalanche, personally seen by the writers, occurred in Coire an t-Sneachda of Cairngorm, when the whole corrie east of Aladdin's Couloir avalanched in one large slide. The length of the *crownwall* was about a kilometre, reaching the summit plateau at two points. The avalanche embraced some popular climbs, including the approach to Jacob's Ladder, where the crown surface was two metres high and also the shallow corrie at the north-eastern end of the cliffs, a popular off-piste ski run. The debris was 400 metres wide and had crossed the lateral moraine on the east side of the corrie, spilling over into the main corrie floor. The trigger for this avalanche was a big fall of very heavy wet snow, falling on a pre-existing wind-slab layer. A Glenmore Lodge party, sleeping in snowholes 30 metres away from the northerly limit of the avalanche as it came down in the night, were undisturbed by it.

Burials

There is widespread belief that complete burials are unusual in Scottish avalanches. In fact, they are quite common; at least 29 more or less complete burials being noted in the accident reports. Many others not resulting in injury are known. These burials have resulted in a number of fatalities due to asphyxia and exposure and others to injuries sustained during the fall.

It is certainly true, however, that avalanche victims in Scotland, alive or dead, typically suffer from injuries due to falling into boulder fields or over cliffs, rather than from burial.

The 24-hour Rule

It is a fact that in Alpine countries most large avalanches (about 80–90%) take place during snowstorms or in the period up to 24 hours immediately thereafter. The comparable figure for Scotland is not known due to the difficulty of observation, but experience suggests that the figure is much lower. Nevertheless, it is a safe assumption that the risk will be higher during and immediately after snowfall; as an example from recent years, the two almost simultaneous avalanche accidents in Coire an t-Sneachda of Cairngorm on January 21, 1978, occurred during a heavy snowfall. A fatal avalanche accident took place on Lochnagar the same day.

However, many Scottish avalanche accidents happen in cold weather long after the last snowfall, due to wind transportation of snow and consequent build-up of slab. Thus, although the 24-hour rule is valid, one does not have a carte blanche to wander unthinkingly on steep slopes after the expiry of that period.

The danger of wet snow avalanches during thaw should be obvious.

Size of Avalanches

A climber or skier may sometimes feel justified in crossing an unsafe slope when it seems that only a small avalanche could result; but, except in the few Scottish cases where the volume of snow has been so overwhelming as to leave the victim little chance of survival, the size of the avalanche bears little relation to the damage done. Some tiny snow slides have caused death or serious injury by carrying climbers over cliffs or into boulder fields or by sweeping them into gullies and then burying them.

Also, the writers have seen an avalanche which travelled no more than 15 m bury a man completely in an upright kneeling position. In one North American survey, about half of the fatal back-country accidents noted travelled no more than 100 metres.

Years of Great Snowfall

Superficially, it would seem that years of great snowfall must produce more avalanche accidents. This is only true, however, in catastrophic avalanche periods in the Alps, when great snowstorms result in disasters to towns and villages. During these periods, on the other hand, access to the high mountains is severely restricted or impossible, resulting in a marked reduction in tourist (i.e. skier and climber) casualties. The notorious avalanche winter of 1950–51 highlighted this point. "Tourist" casualties in Switzerland fell almost to zero.

In Scotland, nearly all potential avalanche victims are "tourists". Admittedly, the problems of access may be less severe, but blocked roads and bad conditions have their effect in keeping people off the hills. A further factor is the effect of heavy snowfall in covering boulder fields. As many Scottish avalanche victims sustain their injuries by hitting rocks during their fall, such heavy snow cover must reduce the level of these injuries.

Thus, even though the total avalanche activity may be greater in a winter of much snowfall, the number of casualties may be lower. The only statistical information available, from the Meteorological Office Snow Survey of Great Britain, tends to support this view.

The Upward Trend

The increase in the number of avalanche accidents in recent years is alarming, but it should be seen in relation to the overall increase in winter accidents, which is in itself merely a reflection of the much increased use of the hills.

Obviously there are yearly anomalies, but generally over the last 15 years, avalanche accidents have represented about 10% of all winter accidents.

There is no room here for smugness amongst experienced climbers. Some of the best known names amongst Scottish mountaineers appear in the accident reports. In these cases, perhaps familiarity breeds the confidence to stretch luck a little too far. In other instances, only inexperience or the grossest kind of foolhardiness could have led to the accident. In one accident on Ben Nevis, a party which had already been carried 170 m in one avalanche went on the same day to attempt another climb, where they were again avalanched; the result in this case was terminal. Some victims have suffered from nothing more than undue bad luck. The four Irish climbers who, on March 26, 1978, were struck by a large, wet-snow avalanche just above the path to the CIC hut on Ben Nevis can hardly be held at fault.

It is worth observing that in almost all cases, sometimes with the exception of cornice collapse, the climber or skier himself has triggered off the avalanche by his presence upon the slope. This is in accord with experience in other countries. As far as records tell, only in two accidents on Ben Nevis have parties been overwhelmed by avalanches from above.

One hazard which may be on the increase is that of shock or pressure waves from low-flying aircraft. The increasing use of Highland mountain areas by high speed low-flying jets may result in future accidents. Tests conducted in France with the cooperation of the French Air Force have established that an aircraft flying at a speed approaching that of sound can produce a pressure increase of 4–6 millibars, equivalent to a new snowfall of about 45 cm. This is more than enough to trigger avalanches in marginal conditions, through overloading of existing weak snow layers. In addition, at least two cases are known where cornice collapses were apparently triggered off by low-flying aircraft.

The question whether a rescue helicopter flying low overhead can trigger an avalanche is a separate one: at the moment, no concrete evidence exists to prove that it can.

The Epidemic Phenomenon

The principle of studying other people's misfortunes has a more direct application: it may warn hillgoers of a potential avalanche epidemic. These interesting phenomena have been in evidence since the early 1970s, when avalanche accidents first began to appear in groups or clusters chronologically. Thus, on January 12–13, 1972, three accidents occurred; on January 19, 1975, four accidents; March 30, 1975, two accidents; March 12–14, 1976, five accidents; January 21, 1978, three accidents; February 19–21, 1978, two accidents; March 16–18, 1980, three accidents; and February 15, 1982, four accidents.

A close attention to press, TV and radio reports may give valuable information as to the location of the accident, slope orientation, type of avalanche and so on. Personal knowledge of recent weather patterns may make it possible to predict whether the risk is widespread or likely to be confined to one area; further epidemic incidents may confirm this. For instance, the two accidents on March 30, 1975, both occurred in the Northern Cairngorms, whereas the incidents on March 12–14, 1976, took place in locations as widely separated as Cairngorm, Lochnagar and Bidean nam Bian. Weather data such as temperature or wind direction may enable a prediction to be made as to the duration of the high risk conditions and any change in orientation of dangerous slopes. Such close monitoring of accident reports by climbers and skiers should not be regarded as ghoulish but as a vital aid to self-preservation.

Three Cairngorm Avalanches

Beinn a'Bhuird, December 28, 1964
"A Chance in a Million"

The latter half of December 1964 was a period of cold and stormy weather in the Southern Cairngorms. The Snow Survey observer at Derry Lodge recorded a heavy cover of new snow between the 13th and 18th, falling on a previous cover lying everywhere at about 900 m, but with large patches down to the 600 m level. A heavy frost, with the mercury falling to −8°C, followed on the 19th. After a slight thaw between the 20th and the 23rd, a further heavy snowfall took place on the hills, with a slight fall of 5 cm at Derry Lodge, at that time a favourite base for climbers in the area, with its striking setting amongst mature pine forest at an altitude of 400 m.

High winds and severe drifting occurred on Christmas Day and Boxing Day, with a moderation of the weather on the next day. On the 28th, the observer recorded "Grey cover at (Survey) Station level."

This was the weather pattern which set the scene for one of the most remarkable avalanche tragedies seen in this country in modern times.

Alexander MacKenzie and Alasdair Murray were both young men involved in the Scouting movement. MacKenzie wanted to complete a mountain walk in the Cairngorms to qualify for his Rambler's

Badge; Murray was to accompany him, and in order to make up a strong party, two university friends of Murray's were invited to come along. The two friends, Robert Burnett and Alexander McLeod, were, like the Scoutmasters, experienced hillwalkers. Neither could have foreseen the fateful consequences of their acceptance. The party met on Sunday, December 27, at Burnett's home in Cowdenbeath and drove the 80 or so miles to Braemar.

About three o'clock that afternoon they set off for Derry Lodge and passed the night at *"Luibeg"*, a bothy adjacent to the Lodge, where the stalker, Bob Scott, was renowned amongst the climbing fraternity as a kindred spirit. At about nine o'clock next morning, the party set out for Beinn a'Bhuird, one of the six highest Cairngorm peaks at 1196 m. The south-western aspect by which the walkers approached it is by no means very steep. Rather than its climbing interest, this side of the mountain is known for the superb, long, but fairly easy descents it gives to the ski mountaineer. Its rugged eastern corries and the remote northern Garbh Coire are quite another matter, giving winter climbing of real difficulty and serious-ness. Conditions were deteriorating by the time the walkers approached the top of Beinn a'Bhuird, like nearly all the Cairngorm summits, an exposed and featureless plateau. A strong north-west wind with snow and low visibility persuaded them to descend from the south top of the mountain, down a small burn running towards the Alltan na Beinne, a tributary of the Quoich Water. Here a pleasant stand of pines affords a sheltered camp site, where the party intended to spend their second night.

The burn by which they were descending is an innocuous looking feature, set on a slope of no more than 30 degrees. The recent, mainly north-west winds blowing across its length, had caused a heavy build-up of snow on the north or true right bank; the other side of the burn, strangely enough, was almost completely clear of snow. The present writer has observed an identical snow build-up at the same spot.

As they descended, Alasdair Murray led the way. Two or three feet of new snow overlay old snow. Robert Burnett tested the snow and "found it firm". This reflects one of the dangerous properties of hard wind-slab; it gives good footing and might in certain circum-stances be confused with snow-ice.

After descending some distance, Murray fell and rolled into the gully; unhurt, he was climbing back to meet his friends on the north side of the burn, when Burnett told him to cross to the other side and meet them at the bottom. This advice very probably saved his life.

Burnett continued down the north side, the others following. All at once, the snow broke away below his feet into a huge slab avalanche. He remembers falling and waving his arms above his head to attract attention. This action may well have been his salvation, for when he regained consciousness (he passed out for an undetermined length of time), he was lying on his back, covered with snow and with both hands extended over his head. Very fortunately, he was able to move his arms and managed to burrow a hole in the snow over his face; his breathing became easier. It is a feature of wind-slab avalanches that, because of the angularity of the debris, air passages may exist quite deep down: one of these passages saved Robert Burnett's life.

Apart from his arms, Burnett was immovably held, and, panicking momentarily, he began to call for help. "No-one came", he later stated, "and it was some time before I was able to control my feelings", words containing a depth of unwritten horror. While Burnett was undergoing this ordeal, Alasdair Murray, who had observed, unharmed, the disappearance of his friends, was making a desperate search. Whether by instinct or by foreknowledge, he did exactly the right thing. He searched, probing the snow with a stick in the hope of finding his friends alive. This kind of quick search by witnesses forms by far the best chance of survival for avalanche burial victims. After half an hour, with their chances of survival now rapidly declining, he decided to go for help.

Help in the Cairngorms is seldom near at hand, except in the crowded northern corries of Cairngorm, and Murray ran for 8 km to the nearest human aid, at Mar Lodge, which at that time was being developed as Scotland's latest ski resort. Police were informed and a rescue party quickly raised, consisting of four Police Mountain Rescue Team members from Braemar and Ballater, climbers, skiers, youth hostellers, gamekeepers and the local Nature Conservancy Officer. As they made their way over the long miles to the scene of the accident, few could have entertained much hope for the survival of any of the buried men. Even had they been unaware of the statistical fact that few people survive a burial for more than two hours, their experience and common sense must have told them that hope bordered on self-deception. This feeling must have been re-inforced by the discovery of Alexander McLeod's body that night. About 4 a.m., as their torch batteries were failing, the rescuers gave up for the night. Reinforcements arrived next morning, when 30 soldiers from Aberdeen joined the rescue attempts. After some hours of fruitless searching, one of the Police rescuers noticed a small hole in the debris, yellowed around the edges. Peering down this, he saw Burnett, alive and calling for help. The feelings of all concerned can be imagined. He was buried between one and two feet deep, but was soon dug out, suffering from frost bite, and evacuated to Braemar. This was at 12.30 p.m. on Tuesday, December 29, after a burial of some 22 hours. This is remarkable not only as the longest recorded survival time in a Scottish avalanche burial, but as one of the longest survivals in full contact with the snow on record anywhere.

Hope must have revived for a live rescue of Alexander MacKenzie, but in truth such a large measure of good fortune was unlikely to be granted twice. Mackenzie was found dead some hours later.

The Beinn a'Bhuird avalanche was of a kind which has unfortunately become typical of Scottish avalanche accidents. It was a large avalanche (some reports say that it was nearly 1 km wide) of hard slab, following high winds and drifting onto a thawed and re-frozen base. With hindsight it is easy to see the classic pattern in the Snow Survey records. It was on an open slope. Did Robert Burnett and the others realise they were on wind-slab? Were they re-assured by the shallow angle of the slope? Looking at the site of the accident, it is easy to see why they imagined themselves to be in no danger. Burnett stated that he thought the avalanche was a "chance in a million." Given the prevalent level of snow and avalanche knowledge at the time, that might have seemed a valid judgement. Of course, we might say, today we would know better; and yet 14 years on, at Christmas 1978, two experienced mountaineers perished in a very similar accident on Braeriach. An avalanche is a capricious foe: on Beinn a'Bhuird, a man lived despite the overwhelming mass of snow released, but no such leniency was shown on Braeriach.

Moreover, as will be seen in the following account, the tiniest of avalanches can wreak injury out of all proportion to its size.

Cairngorm, March 12, 1976

Mountaineers and off-piste skiers operate in a twilight zone of snow safety knowledge. Even in the Alpine countries, which have a highly organised and efficient system of avalanche prediction, no attempt is made by the forecasting service to warn against risk in specific high mountain locations. The forecasts are for inhabited areas and the observations of snow conditions are made at levels where population exists; the obvious exceptions being high level survey stations, such as those at Weissfluhjoch, Davos, and the Col du Lautaret in France.

The prediction services score a high success rate, making accurate forecasts with regard to 80% of major avalanches. The 20% of avalanches not successfully predicted are mainly wind-slab avalanches, which are particularly difficult to forecast. What is difficult for the experts with their specialised knowledge and equipment must be more so for the average mountain-goer, armed only with his eyes, experience, and common sense. In practice, there is no infallible rule of thumb for assessing the stability of a given slope and the mountaineer or skier can scarcely stop every 50 metres to make complicated observations and calculations: at times in serious mountaineering situations, there is no choice but to proceed.

There are, of course, certain criteria to which even most wind-slab avalanches will adhere; they are unlikely to start on a slope under 22°; boulders protruding through the snow will tend to anchor the snow cover; and a concave slope will generally be less prone to avalanche than a convex one. At times, however, wind-slab avalanches do not observe even these conventions.

On the morning of March 12, 1976, several mountaineering groups set out as usual from Glenmore Lodge. The weather forecast gave no cause for special concern, with a 30 knot, south-west wind forecast, backing southerly during the day. Some light snow was predicted. Snow conditions were generally good, with a thawed and re-frozen layer of hard snow above about 800 m. As the day progressed and the weather behaved as forecast, groups on the hill noted a certain amount of soft wind-slab accumulation. Even although this was falling onto a hard base which would provide a good sliding surface, the build-up was not as yet sufficient to warrant anxiety in normal circumstances; only a few centimetres.

About 11.15 a.m., Lodge instructor Jack Thomson had arrived in Coire an t-Sneachda with his group of eight students. He spent some time demonstrating to them the basics of crampon technique, which they practised on a boss of easy angled ice in the floor of the corrie. The party was then split up into four groups of two, so that the students could practice the techniques of climbing in pitches to the plateau, by the steepish slopes of the Goat Track, a normal route of descent for climbers in winter time. The party had already practised snow belaying and set off by parallel routes, fairly close together so that the instructor could check each belay quickly. Proceeding in this way, each student can practise the placement of deadman plates, buried ice axe and snow bollard belays in a realistic, although relatively safe and controlled way. This is a standard method of working at the Lodge, and while Jack Thomson's party was climbing up the Goat Track, other parties were pursuing a similar programme at different locations in the northern corries.

Fred Harper, the Principal of Glenmore Lodge, was working that afternoon in his office. As is normal during winter courses at the Lodge, the Mountain Rescue base radio in his office was on standby. At 2.24 p.m. a call came in from Jack Thomson. His party had been avalanched. One person was injured and help was required. Fred immediately alerted other Lodge groups by radio and several parties were diverted to the scene. At 3.07 p.m. he diverted Roger O'Donovan and his party of eight students from Coire an Lochain to the accident site.

Twenty minutes later, Roger radioed in; on their way from Coire an Lochain over the Fiacaill a'Coire an t-Sneachda to the accident site, his party had also been avalanched; six were hurt, some seriously.

The terrain which Roger's party had to cross was not difficult in mountaineering terms. It was an area of boulder fields interspersed with patches of hard snow and with a slope angle of no more than 20°. They had already passed that way in the morning and noted that there was some slab build-up since then—a few centimetres only. The party was a strong one; perhaps the best group of students Roger had been associated with at the Lodge. Certainly, the weather was not favourable, with a wind of about 30 knots and 25 metres visibility, but again it was by no means bad for the winter Cairngorms. When asked whether they were fit and willing to participate in the rescue, all had answered in the affirmative. Some were doubly motivated, as they had friends in Jack's party, but in any case it is still one of the better traditions of British climbing that help is freely given when other climbers are in trouble. All in all, this party should have had little to fear on their rescue mission, by normal standards. But then, as we have mentioned above, avalanches sometimes do not abide by normal standards.

The climbers were crossing a zone of snow patches interspersed with boulders, following in single file behind the instructor. As the slab deposits had thickened slightly, to about 10 cm, he decided to stop at some boulders a few yards up-slope in order to consider his best route. The present situation did not appear dangerous, but to wander in the limited visibility on to a steeper slope with a bigger build-up might have been unwise.

Then, without warning, the slope was moving beneath them. Roger felt himself hit at knee level by blocks of slab, and with an instinctive quick step up the slope, found himself on safe snow. He turned round, expecting to see his companions laughing and joking about the mini avalanche. No one was to be seen.

The potential seriousness of what had happened was obvious; below and all round were fields of jagged boulders. If the members of the party had been carried far, they might be seriously injured. Following the track of the avalanche down, Roger immediately found two students unhurt. They lined out across the slope, and sweeping downhill soon found the others amongst the boulders between 60 and 100 m below. All six were suffering from injuries. At that point, Roger made his radio call and a major rescue operation was launched. In addition to the ground parties and RAF Rescue helicopter already deployed for the first accident, a second helicopter was summoned to the second accident, as well as other rescuers on foot. Over the next three hours all the casualties were evacuated to Glenmore Lodge where, after examination by a doctor, they were taken by a waiting fleet of ambulances to Raigmore

Hospital, Inverness. In due course all were discharged, after treat-
ment for various injuries including broken arms and legs, with the
exception of Philip Hadfield. He had not at first appeared to be
seriously injured, but had in fact sustained serious head injuries,
despite the wearing of a crash helmet. Tragically, his condition
deteriorated and he died one month after the accident. So the name
of Philip Hadfield was added to the list of those who have lost their
lives going to the aid of others on the Scottish hills; the first to perish
by avalanche.

Several things may be learned by examining this avalanche,
perhaps the most destructive of its size ever recorded in Scotland.
Technically, it was not even large enough to be classed as an
avalanche, the slab which broke away being approximately 5 m wide
and 6–8 m high; it was less than 15 cm thick.

Thus, the mass of snow was very small and injuries were not due
to burial but to the victims hitting rocks. This is typical of Scottish
avalanche accidents and illustrates the danger which results from
even a tiny avalanche if the run-out is dangerous. Injuries sustained
in uncontrolled falls into boulders are usually much more serious
than would seem possible.

Secondly, this slope was studded with boulders which might have
been expected to provide effective peripheral anchorages for the
slab: they did not. Again, this slide took place on an unusually
shallow slope, implying a very weak bond between the slab and
underlying hard layer. The present writer knows of only two other
incidents on slopes of a similar angle; both took place one day on
Stuc a'Chroin and Ben Vorlich, when two parties were avalanched
by soft slab, luckily without injury.

Lastly, we have mentioned that Roger O'Donovan escaped to
safe ground by making a couple of rapid steps upward. He was
probably fortunate in being near the fracture line, but his action was
the correct one. There is often a fraction of a second available for
action before the avalanche takes one's feet away; it may be
possible to jump up-slope to safe terrain above the fracture line or
elsewhere. The climber's adage that it is better to fall off trying to go
up applies here with double force. But the subject of defensive
action by the avalanche victim is a larger one, which will be treated
in a later chapter.

Cairngorm, January 3, 1968
A personal account by one of the authors

The year 1967 died cold and snowy; wintry enough to promise passable climbing on the big cliffs of the Central Cairngorms. My friend, Ian Rowe, suggested a visit to the Shelter Stone Crag, where a great winter route waited. We saw in the New Year lengthily, but the morning of January 2 found us on our way to Aviemore. The A9 was icy and our journey was enlivened by several excursions off-road.

We climbed Cairngorm and on an evening of clear green sky reached St Valery's Refuge. This was a shelter, since destroyed, which stood above Stag Rocks, overlooking the Loch Avon basin in the heart of the Cairngorm range. Our plan was to spend the night here and in the morning descend to the loch, at whose head stands the Shelter Stone Crag. After climbing our route, we would return round the tops to St Valery's. From the refuge, our objective was clearly seen, rather intimidating and improbable.

Night passed indifferently, to reveal a discouraging dawn. A grey light and lowering cloud boded ill. Wind was rising. Nonetheless, the effort was to be made and in grim mood we started our descent of Coire Raibert towards the loch. This corrie, wide and gentle at the top, steepens into a narrow chute for the last 200 metres of its plunge to Loch Avon. We entered the gully at a distinctive group of boulders, to find ourselves straight away with a problem. Rising wind had deposited blown snow to a great depth in the gully. The under-surface was hard and we obviously had a real avalanche risk. As the snow was still powdery and not slabby, and reinforced by the youthful certainty that accidents happened only to other people, we carried on down.

At the loch it was obvious some real weather was brewing. Heavy snow and thickening visibility indicated the onset of a typical Cairngorm blizzard. Climbing plans were abandoned, means of retreat considered. We now found ourselves in a very tricky situation.

On examining the various alternative routes back, we found that none of them recommended themselves. Our route of descent was dangerous and becoming more so by the minute. The steep open slopes on its south side might be safer, but we were unsure of finding the hut again from that direction in the now rapidly deteriorating visibility. Coire Domhain, on the far side of St Valery's, was likely to be equally avalanche-prone; the alternative routes out, by Strath Nethy or even worse, Glen Derry, were long and would mean abandoning our camping gear at St Valery's. At least, from the top of the Raibert gully, we had a landmark and a known back bearing to the refuge. Wisely or not, the decision was made for the gully.

To be caught in a gully by an avalanche is a most unenviable plight. Channelled into a narrow chute, the snow builds up tremendous pressures and burials can be very deep. We knew this, but put it out of our minds as we waded waist and shoulder deep up the hill. Luck was with us and as our landmark appeared, we knew that we would not now fail to find St Valery's. Nevertheless, following our bearing back in the prevailing conditions was not easy, with a strong gale lashing spindrift and falling snow in our faces. The orange marker pole of the hut finally put an end to our trials.

Inside the tiny hut, the routine of bivvy life took over. Into the sleeping bag, brew on, mull over the morning's events. We had time in hand, would stay another night. Tomorrow might be better. We dozed; outside the blizzard howled.

Had we known, we were far from alone that day on the hill. Rescue parties were out searching for three missing climbers. Among the search parties was one led by Eric Langmuir, then Principal at Glenmore Lodge. A respected climber and hospitable soul, his presence drew many of the active mountaineers of the time to the Lodge. When the rescue call had come on this occasion, guests at the Lodge reacted with customary public spirit. Apart from Eric, three noted Scottish climbers, Dave Bathgate, Graham Tiso and Douglas Briggs, answered the call.

This party, tasked to search towards the remote Fords of Avon bothy, found progress impossible beyond the East end of Loch Avon. They decided to climb out of the Loch Avon basin via Coire Raibert. Thus, duty brought these four to the same spot on Loch Avon-side as Ian and I had visited about two hours before.

They were now faced with the same choice as we had been. Rightly assessing the avalanche risk as very high, and not wishing to be caught in the confined gully, they opted for a faint rib on the west side of it. Conditions were now of the worst, with high winds and zero visibility. To avoid becoming separated, they roped up and fought their way slowly up the steepening slope towards St Valery's Hut.

Ian and I dozed on, vaguely conscious of the fading light. Something woke us; the outside world intruded, the door was pushed open and men started crawling in. They wanted to know who we were. No, we were not the people they were looking for, we were Ian Rowe of the SMC.... They squeezed in, one, two, three. Five altogether. A Rescue team—RAF Kinloss men. A very tight squeeze in the hut for seven persons. Anyway, they were just stopping for a brew before heading back to Coire Cas. We commiserated on the thanklessness of rescue work, tut-tutted on the folly of some hill-goers. The rescuers left, heading back towards Coire Cas, the blizzard still seething.

Doze. The door again. Who this time? They were back, the same men. No chance apparently of getting over to Coire Cas. It was too bad. Too much falling snow and spindrift, too difficult to see, or even breathe. Now the situation in the hut was memorable, seven in a space only fit for three. It was cold, but we rested in warm peapod immobility. The Mountain Rescue radio was off for the night.

A few hundred metres away, Eric's party gave up their attempt to reach the hut. A retreat by the route of ascent and a forced bivouac at the Shelter Stone were the dire prospects. Then the avalanche came, swift, without warning; no time for cries, nor for any defensive action. All were swept away in the silent torrent. When it ended, about 100 metres further down, Briggs and Tiso were free. They looked for their companions, buried in the soft slab. Two hands were visible.

Bathgate's face was clear also, so Tiso and Briggs furiously set about digging out Langmuir. He emerged, shaken but not injured. Then, turning to free Dave, to their horror they saw that his free hand had now dropped limply to the snow, his face congested; he had stopped breathing.

Frantic digging ensued and as the upper part of his torso emerged, Dave began to breathe again. The snow had been so tightly packed around his chest as to prevent the movement necessary for breathing. Death had come close.

Now, retreat was a matter of urgency. There were problems.

Graham had injured a leg, while someone else fell through the frozen surface of the loch, becoming soaked to the thighs with icy water. Not the best way to face a sub-zero bivouac. The way to the Shelter Stone was long; it took two hours.

In St Valery's, a bitter morning came. A great frost gripped the plateau and cramped bones reacted wearily. The RAF radio crackled into breakfast tea-time action. "Shelter Stone, this is Glenmore Base." Great difficulty with communication though. The Loch Avon basin is a radio blind spot. We gathered that 16 men, Hamish MacInnes, a team of dogs and a helicopter, were on their way to the Shelter Stone. It seemed some drama was in progress.

We were obviously superfluous to the rescue operation, so started back for Coire Cas. A large yellow rescue helicopter flew overhead, making a brave sight in the blue and white winter landscape. In two minutes it would land at the Shelter Stone. It was all over.

That night in Edinburgh, I met Dave Bathgate and learned the details of the accident. This caused me to reflect somewhat. It was ironic that Dave's party had made a safe decision and nearly met with disaster, while ours had made a risky one and escaped unscathed. There was no cause for self-congratulation in that. Ian and I had been there by choice, and in selecting a dangerous route while other (laborious and inconvenient) alternatives were available, we were entirely typical avalanche fodder. The other party, out in vile conditions on an errand of mercy, sought to minimise the risk.

The other important difference is that we were lucky, while they were not. Clearly it is important to be lucky if one intends taking liberties with avalanches. But in the fulness of time, luck must fail.

Common sense and an intelligently acquired experience must take its place. Allied to these must be a basic knowledge of the theory of snow structure and avalanche release. The ensuing chapter deals with these matters.

II Avalanche Anatomy

Many of the factors influencing avalanche release arise from the behaviour of snow crystals, both in the air and on the ground as part of the snowpack. In this chapter we will look at the formation, deposition and modification of different types of snow crystals, and attempt to relate these changes to the large-scale properties of snow masses.

Snow in the Air examines the formation and properties of the main types of snow crystal.

Snow on the Ground considers how the main types of snow crystals are deposited in a snowpack, and how they are subsequently modified. The formation of loose snow avalanches is examined.

Snowpack Structure considers the layering of the snowpack and looks at the factors relating to the release of slab avalanches. The formation and behaviour of cornices is examined.

Snow in the Air

The size and shape of a snow crystal is largely determined by the conditions of temperature and humidity that it experiences, both at its point of formation and during its journey to the ground. The different forms are all constructed on a hexagonal plan, but include a wide variety of shapes such as needles, stellar crystals, columns and plates.

These forms are typical of crystals at their point of formation in a cloud, and in fairly calm conditions they can fall to the ground more or less intact, either individually, or as clusters of several crystals (snowflakes). We will include all these forms in the single term **new snow**.

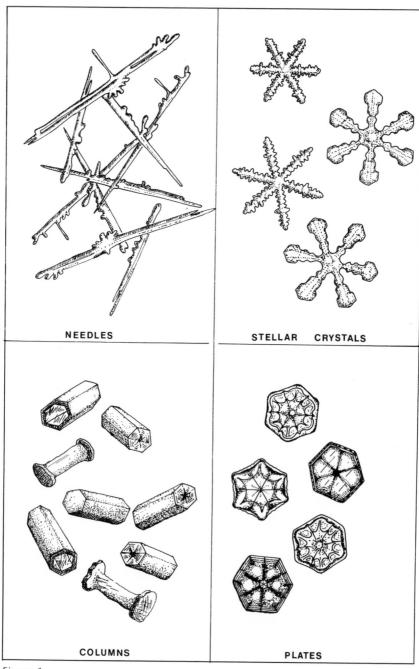

NEEDLES

STELLAR CRYSTALS

COLUMNS

PLATES

Figure 1

Whilst falling to the ground these "new" snow crystals can be modified in various ways.

If the snow is falling in winds above, say, 15 knots, the crystals will be damaged to some degree, and we will call all extensively wind-damaged crystals **broken crystals**.

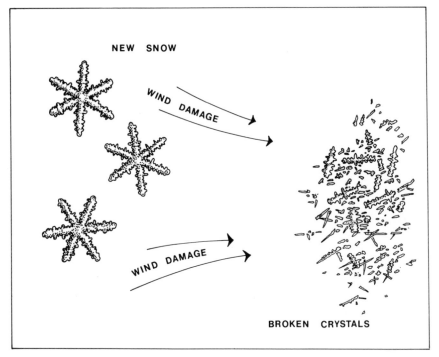

Figure 2

The more delicate stellar crystals are particularly prone to wind damage. Meteorological records for Cairngorm summit (1245 m) indicate that for the period October 25, 1978, to May 31, 1979, only one day in six had a mean daily windspeed below 20 knots. This suggests that broken crystals are likely to be the predominant form in the Scottish hills.

In winter a thick, white crust of rime-ice often forms on the windward side of boulders, ski-lift pylons, and other exposed objects. This is where tiny, supercooled water-droplets in the air freeze onto the surface of the object concerned. Snow crystals can be involved in a similar process, and they in turn can become encrusted in a coating of rime, both in the cloud and whilst falling to the ground. This riming is particularly likely with the turbulence associated with mountain barriers or the passage of cold fronts, and the original form of the crystal may be completely obscured by the encrustation of rime. These heavily rimed pellets are called Graupel, and are a common and uncomfortable component of Scottish winter storms. We will call all extensively rimed forms **rimed crystals**.

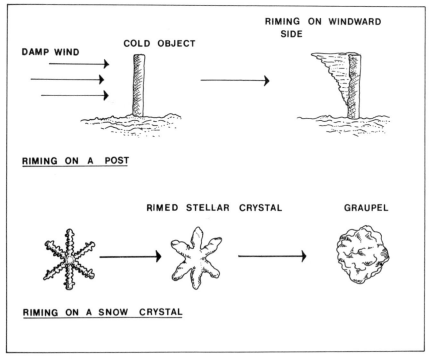

Figure 3

If the air temperature near the ground is above 0°C, some melting will affect all the previous types, and will produce **wet snow**. We will not look closely at the fate of falling wet snow, since the thaw with which it is associated is likely to have its greatest effect on the already existing snowpack.

Any snowfall is likely to include several of these different snow types simultaneously, and a hand lens will reveal this variety among the crystals caught on a dark jacket sleeve during a storm.

If we ignore wet snow, we are left with three main categories:

New snow   **Broken crystals**   **Rimed crystals**.

Each of these can be deposited and subsequently modified in different ways, and we will consider this in the next section.

Snow on the Ground

New Snow

New snow will remain unbroken during its journey to the ground only in relatively still, cold air and in these conditions it will tend to be deposited as a fairly uniform blanket of light, fluffy powder snow. This type of snowfall is more commonly seen in the valleys than on exposed mountains, but when it does occur on the tops, the snow will often adhere to the faces of crags and other steep slopes. This is possible because the more feathery crystals can intermesh and provide enough cohesion to support the very low density snow.

Equitemperature Metamorphism

It is a basic property of snow crystals that there is a higher vapour pressure at their points than at their hollows. The practical effect of this is that a net transfer of material occurs, ice being moved from the points to the hollows. This leads to a conversion of complex, branched crystals to more simple, rounded ones.

It should be noted that the transfer of material is by **sublimation** which involves a direct transition from ice to water vapour or back again. Melting or liquid water does not occur.

This process, converting complex branched crystals to more simple rounded ones is called **Equitemperature Metamorphism (ET met)** and will affect all snow crystals in non-thawing snowpacks. The simplification of the crystals is reflected in the alternative name of **Destructive Metamorphism**.

B

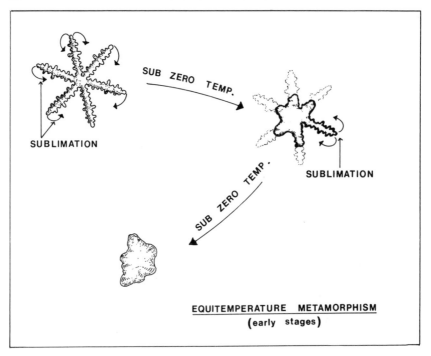

SUB ZERO TEMP.

SUBLIMATION

SUBLIMATION

SUB ZERO TEMP.

SUB ZERO TEMP.

EQUITEMPERATURE   METAMORPHISM
(early stages)

Figure 4

The crystals in our uniform blanket of new snow will be affected by *ET met* and will undergo the change of shape shown in Diagram 4. This means that some of the cohesion provided by the intermeshing crystals is lost, and the snow becomes more free-flowing. This phenomenon allows an explanation of the observed fact that the best powder snow skiing often occurs some time after the snow has fallen—the delay allowing *ET met* to act on the snow.

If the blanket of new snow is poised on a relatively steep slope, this loss of cohesion—like converting a pile of cornflakes to rice grains—can cause a dry, loose snow avalanche. Such loose snow avalanches start with the movement of a few crystals, but a chain reaction ensues, which can ultimately lead to a huge avalanche.

In Scotland, powder snow avalanches are usually small, and the main risk would be of a climber or skier being dislodged but in bigger mountains powder snow avalanches can be very large, and if their speed reaches about 70 km per hour, they can become airborne—a near explosive process which produces a destructive shock wave and a suffocating cloud of snow dust.

There are no definite records of airborne powder avalanches in Scotland, but it is not difficult to imagine that under suitable conditions, some of the long steep slopes of Creag Meagaidh or Ben Nevis might produce them.

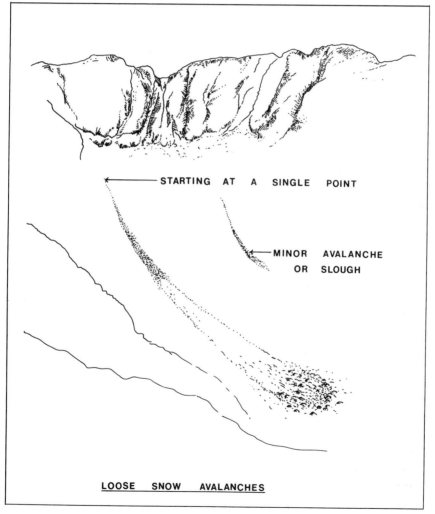

Figure 5

If our mass of "new" snow survives the initial loss of cohesion without avalanching, *ET met* will continue, but will have a stabilising effect, for the transfer of material from convexities will tend to build up a network of bonds between adjacent snow grains.

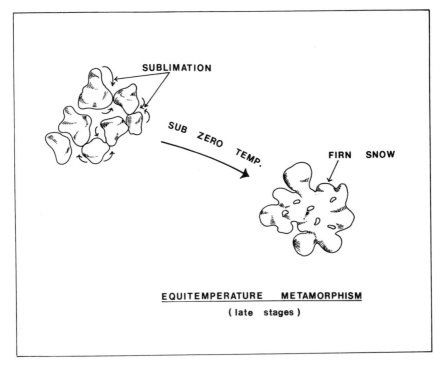

SUBLIMATION

SUB ZERO TEMP.

FIRN   SNOW

EQUITEMPERATURE   METAMORPHISM

(late   stages)

Figure 6

If the snow is subjected to extensive *ET met* the end product will be a strong structure of *firn snow* where all the grains are interlinked. *Firn snow* is the normal stable snow of Alpine regions, but is not quite as common in Britain because of the greater degree of melting and refreezing that is likely to occur. The speed with which *ET met* proceeds depends on temperature—near 0°C the metamorphism is rapid; at −40°C it ceases altogether. This means that falls of "new" snow may constitute a threat of loose snow avalanches for long periods when the temperature is very low.

Temperature Gradient Metamorphism

This process of *ET met* affects all snowpacks not subject to melting, but if a strong temperature gradient is also present, a second process called **Temperature Gradient Metamorphism (TG met)** may eclipse it.

In any snowpack in temperate regions the insulating effect of snow keeps the ground surface at or very near 0°C, this fact allowing the survival of many plants through the winter. However, the snow surface may be very much colder than this, so a gradient of temperature is set up through the snowpack.

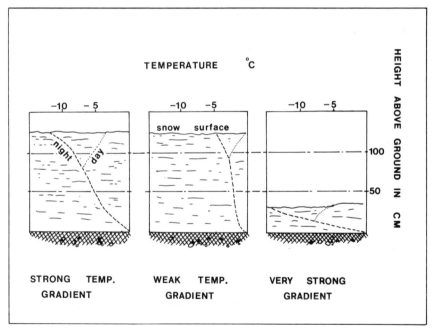

Figure 7

The strongest gradients (i.e. the maximum rate of temperature change with depth) occur when low air temperatures are in conjunction with shallow, unconsolidated snowpacks. When these conditions prevail for several days, there is a vertical migration of water vapour through the snowpacks and a particular stepped and faceted kind of crystal begins to be built up. These crystals are called **Temperature Gradient grains** and if the strong gradient persists for, say two weeks, they can be formed as fragile, hollow cup-crystals, or depth hoar.

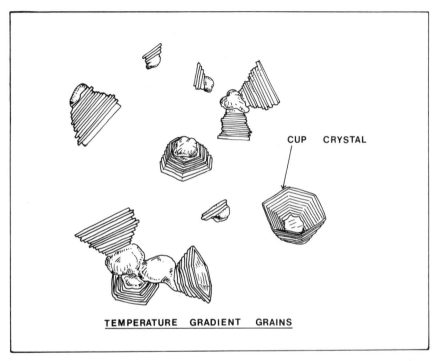

CUP CRYSTAL

TEMPERATURE GRADIENT GRAINS

Figure 8

These present a major threat in continental climates, where a layer of depth hoar can form in shallow early season snowpacks during long cold spells, and form the critical weak layer that will ultimately release a slab avalanche.

However, it has not been demonstrated that *TG grains* have played a significant part in Scottish avalanches. There are several possible reasons for this apparent absence of major *TG met*.

(1) The typical Scottish winter involves too many rapid fluctuations of temperature to allow a stable gradient to be established over a number of weeks.

(2) We do not often see the prolonged hard frosts which would lead to a very strong gradient.

(3) Most snowfalls in the Scottish mountains are windpacked, and such compact slabs may not allow the easy migration of water vapour that would encourage *TG met*.

There is little doubt that in cold conditions *TG met* does occur in Scottish snowpacks, but it seems to be overshadowed in importance by other influences, to such an extent that we will largely ignore its effect. However, it should be noted that with the exception of Langmuir's work, little systematic observation of Scottish mountain snowpacks has been made by observers familiar with *TG met* and its recognition, so it is not impossible that further work might lead to a re-assessment of this evidence.

Melt–Freeze Metamorphism

Both *ET* and *TG met* are processes which occur in the absence of any melting in the snow pack. If a cycle of melting and re-freezing affects the snow, then the dominant process is called **Melt–Freeze Metamorphism (MF met)**.

In thaw conditions practically all snow crystals are reduced to rounded ice grains surrounded by a film of liquid water. A subsequent freeze will cement these grains together into a very strong structure, and a cycle of melting and freezing will produce large, coarse *Melt–Freeze grains*. (See p. 34, fig. 9.)

During the melting phase each grain becomes lubricated by a film of water, and in heavy thaws the snow forms a slurry, which can lead to wet, loose snow avalanches. These avalanches are very destructive, particularly if channelled, because of the density of the snow, but their likelihood is often clearly indicated by the very wet nature of the snow underfoot. Such an avalanche, where a heavy thaw acted on a recent new snowfall, led to the serious avalanche in Great Gully, Buachaille Etive Mór, during February 1970.

The greatest melting is produced by warm, wet winds and by rainfall percolating the snow. It will surprise no one familiar with the Scottish climate that these influences are much more important than is solar heating.

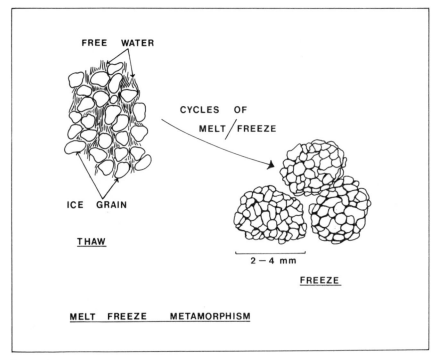

Figure 9

When freezing occurs a strong, rigid material ideal for cramponing is formed—most British climbers would call this névé. The mechanism of melting and refreezing is a most important one for stabilising the snowpack in Scotland during winter. In high, Alpine regions, which lack our variable climate, *Equitemperature Metamorphism* is the major stabilising influence.

Broken Crystals

Wind Transport of Snow

Winds in excess of about 15 knots will cause appreciable damage to the new snow crystals, both by turbulence in the air and by trundling them along the ground. The carrying capacity of a wind is largely dependent on its speed, so the broken crystals will tend to be dumped in areas where the wind is decelerating. These areas will be accumulation zones and are the places where a person might try to seek shelter from the full force of the wind. They include lee slopes, corries and minor hollows.

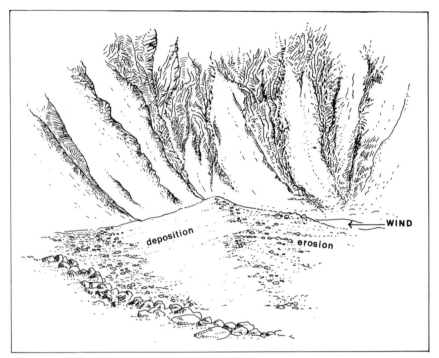

Figure 10

The corresponding areas exposed to the full power of the wind are erosion zones where snow can be stripped away and re-transported. A particular slope can be an accumulation zone with, say, north-east winds, but will become an erosion zone with south-west winds. These wind shifts may happen in a couple of hours, and cause a dramatic re-distribution of the snow cover. (See p. 36, fig. 11.)

When the broken crystals are dumped in an accumulation zone, their pulverised nature allows them to pack much more closely than new snow would, and they become welded into a compact cohesive slab of **wind-slab**. The simpler snow crystals such as needles, can pack in a similar way without being extensively broken.

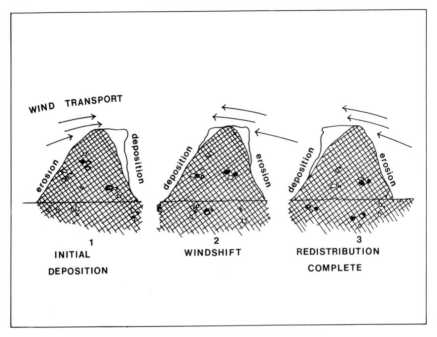

WIND TRANSPORT

erosion   deposition

deposition   erosion

deposition   erosion

1
INITIAL
DEPOSITION

2
WINDSHIFT

3
REDISTRIBUTION
COMPLETE

Figure 11

Wind-slab is much denser than new snow; it will fracture into blocks when broken, and has a chalky, unreflective surface since the sparkling crystals have been largely crushed.

The surface is sometimes gently rippled, and the snow can squeak when walked on, as the crystals rub together, although little internal structure can be seen—the wind-slab has a rather homogenous, felt-like appearance.

The slab exists in a wide range of hardnesses, related to the wind speed. In light winds a very soft slab forms, whilst higher winds will usually produce a more rigid and much denser slab. The continuous spectrum of hardnesses is arbitrarily divided into *soft-slab* and *hard-slab* by whether or not the snow surface can support the weight of a person on foot.

There is some evidence that winds over 60 knots create such widespread turbulence, that wind-slab is dissipated as fast as it is formed, except in sheltered pockets, but this should not be relied upon to indicate "safe" conditions.

Metamorphism of Wind-slab

Wind-slab will be affected by the different types of metamorphism in a similar way to new snow.

ET metamorphism will tend to increase the strength and rigidity of soft-slabs and may increase the adhesion of such a slab to the layers of snow beneath it. The progress of *ET met* will be accompanied by settling, but to a lesser degree than occurs with new snow, since the initial soft-slab has a much greater density than does new snow. Hard-slab is similarly affected, but with a less pronounced settling still.

The release of free water in the snow pack by a thaw will reduce the strength of the wind-slab and may loosen its adhesion to lower layers of snow. This will be looked at in more detail in the section on slab avalanches.

A freeze following the thaw will have the effect of strengthening the slab, and improving its adhesion to any lower layers, and this is probably the main influence in limiting slab avalanche danger in Scotland.

Wind Erosion

In non-thawing conditions, existing snowpacks in exposed locations can be eroded by the wind, and the broken crystals produced will be carried and re-deposited as wind-slab in an accumulation zone. Evidence of this erosion includes blowing spindrift, wind carved ridges called *sastrugi*, and raised footprints and ski-tracks, where the compacted snow in a track has been able to resist the eroding wind, but the surrounding snow has not.

When any of these signs are seen one can assume that nearby accumulation zones have been loaded with wind-slab.

As long as the temperature remains below zero, a particular snowfall may be deposited, eroded and re-deposited elsewhere, a number of times. This means that wind-slab may be built up on a site **in the complete absence of a fresh snowfall**.

After a period of *MF metamorphism*, the coarse, icy, melt-freeze grains are much more resistant to erosion and widespread wind transport is then unlikely. (See pp. 38 and 39, figs. 12a and 12b.)

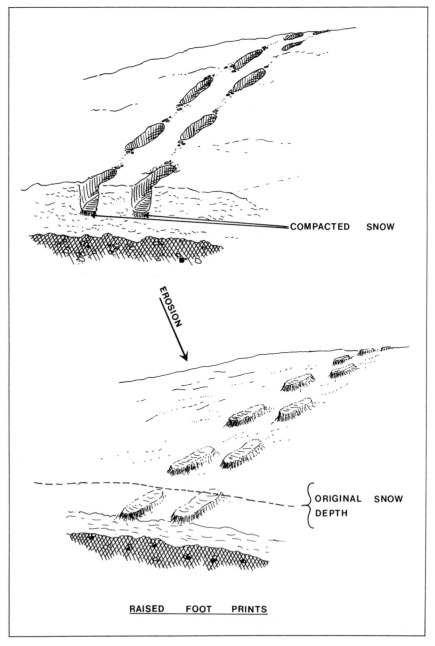

COMPACTED SNOW

EROSION

ORIGINAL SNOW DEPTH

RAISED FOOT PRINTS

Figure 12a

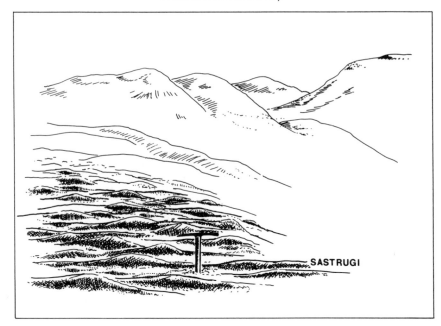

Figure 12b

Rimed Crystals

Our damp, windy climate encourages riming, so many crystals will be affected to some degree, but the heavily rimed forms such as *graupel* are less common than wind broken snow. Thus, *graupel* pellets will often collect at the foot of gullies or hollows, but they can be incorporated in the snowpack as a layer. In these circumstances, their rounded shape makes them very resistant to all types of metamorphism, and so they can remain as loose grains, unattached to adjacent snow layers. The *graupel* pellets can exist in the snowpack for weeks without any major change, and only a major melt-freeze episode will bind them firmly.

These layers of unconsolidated, rimed crystals are a common factor in Scottish slab-avalanches. This will be examined more fully in the section on that topic.

The last two sections have attempted to describe the formation and modification of different types of snow. Their inter-relationships can be shown by a diagram. (See p. 40.)

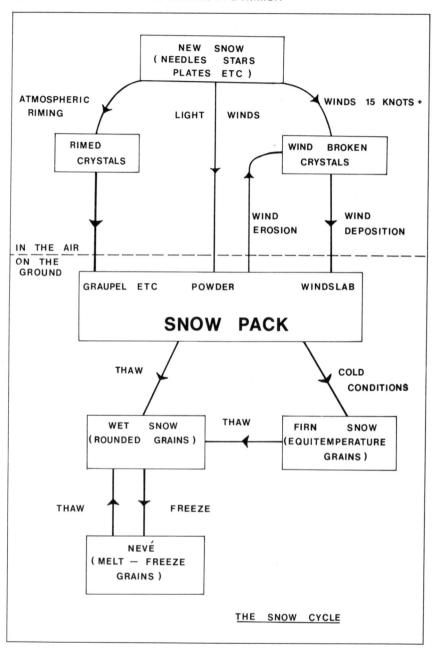

Figure 13

However, this only looks at the behaviour of a substantially uniform mass of snow. Many of the factors which contribute to slab-avalanches arise from the layering and variability of the snowpack, and these complexities will be examined in the next section.

Snowpack Structure

As we saw in the previous section, loose snow avalanches occur when the cohesion between individual grains or crystals breaks down, so the process can be largely understood by examining the properties and changes of the individual grains themselves. For instance, a powder avalanche may release when *ET metamorphism* reduces the intermeshing of new snow crystals; wet loose snow avalanches occur when melt-water breaks down the adhesion of one grain to another.

However, this microscopic approach is not sufficient to account for the occurrence of slab avalanches, and we must look to the varying properties of the large-scale structure of the snowpack to provide further explanation.

For slab avalanches, one of the most important features is the layering of the snowpack. In a continental climate, this stratification may reflect the whole season's weather history, with an identifiable layer for each snowfall, but in Scotland it is fairly common for a major thaw to merge together all but the most distinctive layers into an apparently uniform mass.

The influence of layering, and of other contributory factors, is best examined in the context of the basic mechanics of slab avalanche release.

Figure 14   **EQUILIBRIUM OF A SLAB**

In simple terms a slab will release when the component of its weight (W) acting down the slope exceeds the resistance (R) which anchors the slab to its surroundings. R is the sum of various components, but the most important factor is usually the adhesion between a slab, and the snow or ground beneath it. When W exceeds R the slab will fracture, and usually release. The fractures will be underneath the slab, across its top and along its sides. Of these, the most useful to consider are the fractures at the *crownwall* and at the bed surface.

The *crownwall* is almost always perpendicular to the bed surface, and is usually arched across the slope. The presence of such a break-off wall is the definitive feature of slab avalanches, since the debris is often so broken in its fall as to contain no recognisable blocks.

The bed surface is most commonly found between the slab and a lower layer of snow (a surface avalanche) but it can occur at the ground surface (a full depth avalanche). The fracture across the lower edge of the slab usually leaves an indefinite, ledge-like wall. This is sometimes called the *"stauchwall"*.

These features are shown in the diagram opposite.

Wind-slab avalanches are the greatest threat to mountaineers and skiers in Scotland, and we have discussed in some detail the formation and deposition of wind-slab. However, wind-slab in itself is not a threatening phenomenon—before it, or any other type of snow, becomes a slab avalanche, several other contributory factors must be present simultaneously. The main contributory factors can be broadly classified as follows:

(1) Those related to the accumulation of snow.
(2) Those related to the terrain.
(3) Those related to the presence of weak layers in the snow.
(4) Those related to the triggering of the avalanche.

Each of these will be looked at in turn.

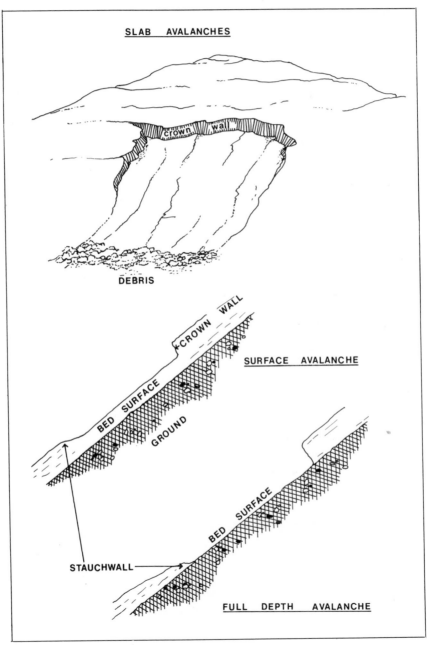

Figure 15

Accumulation

The likelihood of an avalanche occurring is closely related to the rate of accumulation of snow and the thickness to which slabs are built up. If all other things could be kept equal, a deep wind-slab would be much more likely to avalanche than a shallow one, since the increased weight would put a much greater strain on the anchors of the slab.

In (a) the weight (W) of the shallow slab is much less than the possible resistance (R). The slab is stable.

In (b) the weight of the deep slab is now greater and W is approximately equal to R. The slab is unstable, and is poised on a hairtrigger. A further increase in W by a further build-up of snow, or a decrease in R by a weakening of the slab's anchors, will release an avalanche.

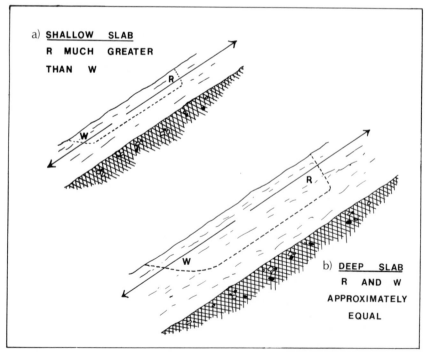

Figure 16

This is of course over-simplification of a complex state of affairs, but it leads to a conclusion that is borne out by the available statistics. **Almost all large, dry slab-avalanches follow a period of heavy snowfall or considerable drifting**, when thick wind-slabs will be built up.

This is particularly well seen in the records of avalanche *'epidemics'*, such as the one of January 21, 1978, where three separate avalanche accidents followed a period of heavy snowfall and drifting.

The thickness of a slab also influences the severity of any resulting avalanche. Normally, anything shallower than 15 cm is not considered to present a great risk, but the funnelling effect of gullies, and the local variations in slab thickness can make this judgement a very unreliable one.

Terrain

Slab avalanches most commonly start on slopes of an inclination between 30° and 45°. This is much steeper than those most commonly skied, but is just the type of slope that a winter mountaineer will often frequent. On slopes steeper than 45°, there is not the build-up of snow to give very large avalanches, but even a small avalanche on such terrain can cause a very serious fall.

A mass of snow is not absolutely rigid, but will deform slightly under its own weight. On a uniform slope the tension tends to increase with height, on an undulating slope regions of tension and compression occur at convexities and concavities respectively.

Figure 17 overleaf illustrates these effects.

Regions where the snow surface is under tension are more likely to develop the transverse fractures that can lead to the *crownwall* fracture of a slab avalanche. It is common for such fractures to occur in or just below the tension zone associated with a convexity.

A hard, smooth layer forms an ideal bed surface for a slab avalanche. Full depth avalanches often run on smooth rock slabs, or flattened long grass, partial depth ones on layers of hard icy snow. The first snowfall of a season will often be firmly anchored to an angular boulder-field, but there are isolated reports of avalanches in

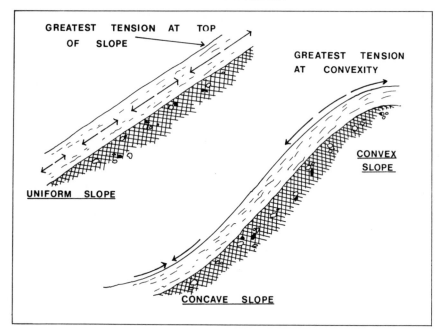

GREATEST TENSION AT TOP OF SLOPE

GREATEST TENSION AT CONVEXITY

CONVEX SLOPE

UNIFORM SLOPE

CONCAVE SLOPE

Figure 17

these circumstances, possibly due to a layer of ice concealing the irregularity of the boulders. A leading Scottish climber was injured in such an avalanche on the back wall of Coire Cas one early November in the late seventies.

Weak Layers

When a slab avalanche has occurred, one of the remarkable features is often the flatness and regularity of the bed surface. This suggests that the fracture has taken place at a definite level in the snowpack, and in fact the bed surface can often be shown to correspond to a definite weak layer in the snowpack, or a distinct lack of adhesion between adjacent layers. Sometimes the weak layer is a stratum of fragile or unconsolidated crystals in the snowpack. A layer of ball-bearing like *graupel* or of fragile cup crystals are clear examples, and a similar problem is caused when crystals of surface hoar are buried.

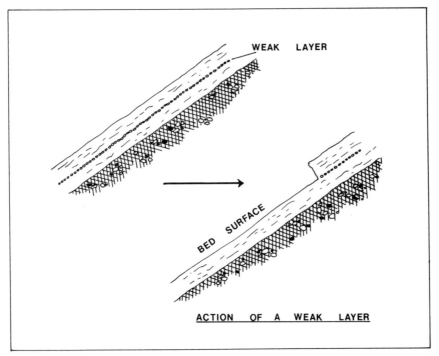

Figure 18

Surface hoar forms on still, cold nights and is the solid equivalent of dew. It is deposited on the snow surface as brittle, erect plates. These provide delightful skiing but if a subsequent snowfall buries them, the fragile plates form a very weak foundation, which is very hard to detect. A spate of fairly small avalanches in the Cairngorms in December 1977 ran on a base of buried surface hoar.

If a rigid hard-slab is laid down over much softer snow, the snow will settle under the influence of *ET met*, and leave the hard-slab poised over a hollow, empty layer. (See p. 48, fig. 19.) This is a very dangerous state of affairs. Any major difference of hardness, wetness or crystal size between adjacent layers usually indicates a poor adhesion between these layers, so for instance a new slab, laid over a hard icy base, will rarely adhere satisfactorily. In thaw conditions, ice layers collect the meltwater and lubricate the release of the slab above.

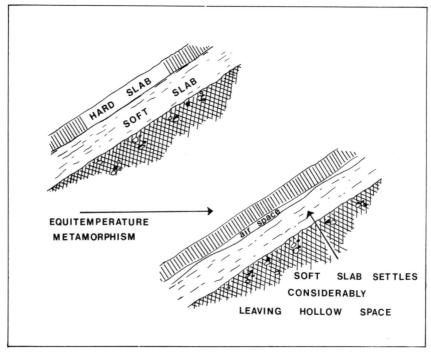

Figure 19

This is most common in full depth avalanches, where the melt-water lubricates the bed surface on, say, a rock slab. This is the mechanism of the full depth wet slab that often occurs on the Great Slab of Coire an Lochain during the spring thaw. (See figure opposite.)

Often, no clear discontinuity is seen in the snowpack, but blocks will fracture on a definite line. This probably corresponds to a change in snowfall intensity, wind direction or temperature. Storms that start warm and become colder are likely to produce more stable slabs than those that start cold and become warmer, since in the latter case, cold brittle crystals, which do not readily adhere to the lower snow layers, are overloaded by more compact, denser snow.

The identification of weak layers in the snow-cover is one of the most effective ways of assessing avalanche risks. We will examine this in more detail in a later chapter. (See Chapter III, p. 59, et seq.)

WET SLAB AVALANCHE COIRE AN LOCHAIN

MELTWATER LUBRICATES BED SURFACE

SMOOTH ROCK SURFACE

FULL DEPTH
WET SLAB
AVALANCHE

Figure 20

Trigger

The trigger of a slab avalanche is the increase in load or decrease in resistance that breaks the bonds between the slab and the main slope.

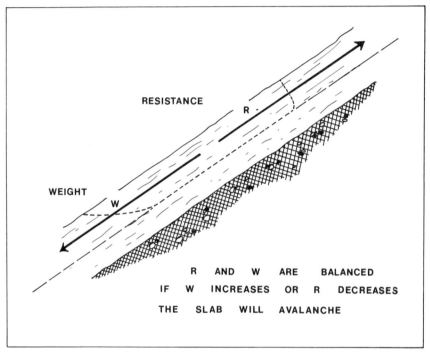

Figure 21

Internal triggering (a reduction of R, resistance) can be caused by the collapse of a layer of fragile crystals, or the destruction of the cohesion of the lowest layers of a slab by meltwater. Any rise in temperature will normally weaken the anchors of a slab, even if melting does not occur.

External triggers usually involve an increase in the loading of the slab (an increase in W). Possible triggers are the weight of extra snow or rainfall, a cornice collapse, or the weight of a climber or skier. The shock waves associated with explosives or sonic booms can initiate fractures, but stories of the similar effect of a loud shout are likely to be apocryphal. Most slab avalanches that cause injury are triggered by their victims' disturbance of the slope.

So, the four critical factors which contribute to the release of a slab avalanche are:

	Accumulation	Terrain	Weak Layer	Trigger	
Mnemonic:	All	These	Will	Trigger	Avalanches
	c	e	e	r	
	c	r	a	i	
	u	r	k	g	
	m	a		g	
	u	i	L	e	
	l	n	a	r	
	a		y		
	t		e		
	i		r		
	o				
	n				

A particular example should show the way in which these different factors interact.

A Case History

Towards the end of March 1975 an Arctic airstream influenced Scotland, with widespread snowfall. Extracts from the weather forecast for the Cairngorm Plateau, and from the observed values for Glenmore Lodge at 350 m, are shown, together with relevant weather maps, overleaf.

March 30 was a weekend and a Bank Holiday. Two climbers were in Coire an Lochain, and were crossing the upper part of the *Great Slab* in order to do a climb in the vicinity of the *Vent*, when they were caught in a large slab avalanche perhaps 200 metres wide, and of maximum height of 1·5 metres at the crown face. They were carried down about 180 metres to just above the lochan, and were lucky to escape with relatively minor leg injuries.

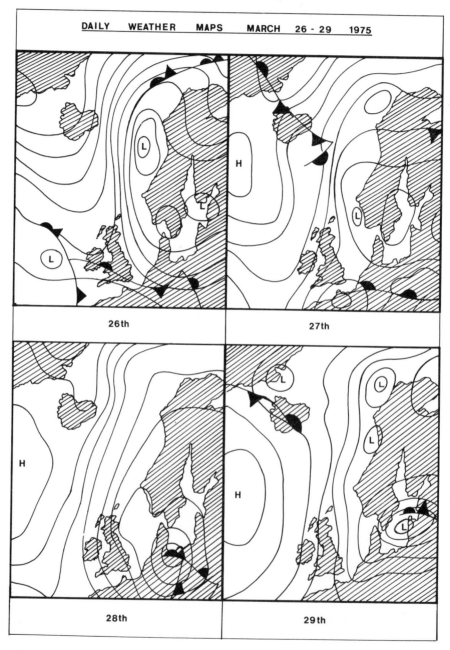

Figure 22

	Forecast for 1000 m			Observed at 350 m			
1975	Snowfall	Wind	Freezing level	Precipitation (water equivalent)	Wind	Temperature °C Min	Max
25 Mar	Yes	E or NE Strong	All levels	4 mm	W 8 kt	−1·2	0·9
26 Mar	Frequent	N or NW 40 kt, gusting 60	All levels	4 mm	NNE 7 kt	−6·5	2·1
27 Mar	Heavy showers	N 15–25 kt Blizzard	All levels	11 mm	SW 5 kt	−3·6	3·2
28 Mar	Frequent showers	NW 10 kt	300 m or lower	2 mm	NE 7 kt	−5·2	0·3
29 Mar	Showers	N 25 kt	300 m	9 mm	NW 8 kt	−2·6	3·6
30 Mar	No	NW 10–20 kt increasing	All levels rising to 300 m by afternoon	3 mm	W 6 kt	−2·9	0·8

Many of the differences between forecast and observed values are due to the difference in altitude, and the difficulties of extrapolating observations from 350 to 1000 m. The actual weather experienced at 1000 m is likely to be somewhere between the two sets of values. The most notable features are:

(1) Consistent sub-zero temperatures above 1000 m.
(2) Considerable precipitation (as snow).
(3) Winds 15–30 knots (excluding gusts) at 1000 m, varying between the north-east and north-west quadrants.

Let us look at how the various factors contributed to the likelihood of this avalanche.

1 Accumulation

Coire an Lochain is situated on the edge of the Cairngorm Plateau— an ideal collecting area for snow which can then drift into the corrie to produce the very deep slabs observed in this case.

THE VENT

AVALANCHE   GREAT   SLAB   COIRE   AN   LOCHAIN

MARCH   30th   1975

Figure 23

There had been considerable snowfall in the preceding week, and the combination of consistently low temperatures and winds of 15–30 knots indicated considerable drifting of the snow, with a widespread build up of wind-slab. One would expect this to be most widespread on south-west and south-east slopes, from the observed wind directions in the northerly quadrants, but this prediction ignores local variations in wind direction. Evidently, many slopes were being loaded with wind-slab, as the avalanche was on a north-west facing slope (GR 984027), and indeed, observers had reported widespread avalanche risk during the preceding days.

2 Terrain

The Great Slab is a large, uniform rock-slab set at 30–35° within the range of angle where large avalanches commonly occur.

The cold weather in the last week of March had been preceded by a warmer, wetter spell. On March 21 the freezing level was above 1700 m, with rain and high winds, so all existing snowpacks would be subject to a thaw. The subsequent freeze would produce the hard, icy snowpack that we have discussed in the section on *MF metamorphism.*

This would provide a perfect bed surface for a slab avalanche to slide on.

3 Weak Layers

An examination of the crown surface and the layers beneath on the day after the avalanche revealed the following section. (See p. 56, fig. 24.)

The icy bed surface was covered in a 1cm thick layer of very fragile snow pellets (possibly *graupel*). The very deep wind-slab above this was almost uniform, with a slight change of texture at half height. This suggests that the wind-slab was laid down by just one or two snowfalls or bouts of drifting.

4 Trigger

The continued build-up of wind-slab would be overloading the weak layers beneath. Over the preceding days the wind-slab would be subjected to increasing tension as the whole slab tended to creep down hill under the force of gravity. The final trigger was provided by the climbers traversing onto the slope. The fracture at the crown surface crossed their tracks.

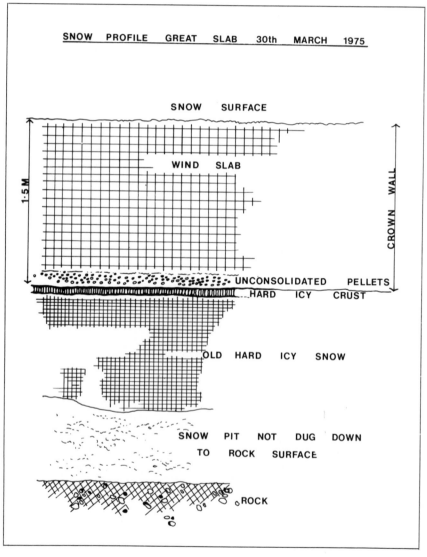

Figure 24

This is an unusually clear-cut case, where all the contributory factors seem to point toward a high avalanche risk. This is underlined by the fact that a little later on the same day of March 30, a party of skiers was avalanched near the top of the March Burn (GR 978010) on a west-facing slope. It would be reasonable to assume that the features of the snowpack were similar in the two instances.

The second party also noted a sudden increase in temperature, shortly before the avalanche occurred. This could reduce the strength of the anchors of the slab, and provide further encouragement for it to avalanche.

Cornices

When a wind blows over a ridge or a crag edge, a kind of cylindrical eddy is formed on the lee slope. If the wind is carrying broken crystals of snow, they will tend to be deposited in this eddy as wind-slab. However, because of the circular motion of the air in this eddy, the wind-slab is not laid down as a plane surface, but instead forms the familiar shell-like shape of a cornice.

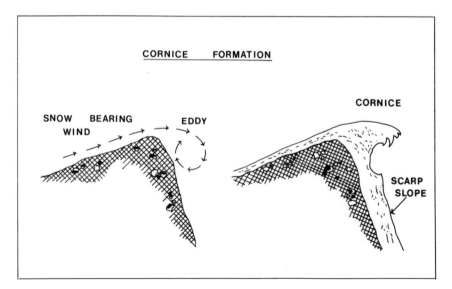

Figure 25

Just below the eddy the snow is deposited as a normal slope of wind-slab. This uniform wind-slab is called the *scarp slope* and is always found in association with a freshly formed cornice. It is often a very soft slab.

Cornices can overhang as much as 10 metres and are intrinsically unstable. They are most dangerous when freshly formed, or when subject to heavy thaw conditions. In these conditions it can be very risky to venture into a gully which is corniced above.

Avoiding a cornice to one side is always advisable, but if a frontal assault is necessary, the narrowest point should be crossed, and a sound belay taken. Tunnelling is aesthetic but rarely advisable. In February 1979, five men were carried down Number 5 gully on Ben Nevis, when the cornice collapsed whilst being tunnelled.

Many mountain accidents are caused by cornice collapse, or falls from the rotten snow of a cornice. One of the most insidious cases can be when drifting snow rapidly builds up a dangerous cornice and *scarp slope* on the last 30 metres of an otherwise unaffected slope.

Another hidden hazard is caused when a cornice begins to sag under its own weight. This builds up tensions within the snow, and causes the likely fracture line to be much further back from the edge than one would expect from the configuration of the ground beneath.

It is wise to give a cornice a wide berth on the windward side to avoid this possibility.

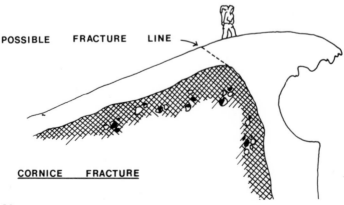

POSSIBLE   FRACTURE   LINE

CORNICE   FRACTURE

Figure 26

III Improving the Odds

Avalanche Awareness

"Avalanches are dangerous natural phenomena that affect other people." So runs the conventional view.

It is very difficult to accept that one might be personally involved in an avalanche, but this admission is a vital first step to an avalanche awareness that might be life saving.

Carrying the Right Gear

Nowhere is this awareness harder to develop than in the carrying of safety equipment in the party. It is noted elsewhere that axes and the heels of skis are far less effective for excavating a buried victim than even the most rudimentary shovel, yet how many British parties carry such a lightweight shovel?

Similarly, probing with axes and normal ski sticks is far less effective than the use of purpose-built collapsible probes.

Ideally, every person would carry a probe, and every fourth person a shovel, though this is perhaps too much to ask.

Ski mountaineers are particularly at risk, because their sport takes them into snow accumulation areas, and they can arrive rapidly in a dangerous situation. It would be wise for those involved in serious ski-tours to carry a transceiver. These are invaluable aids to avalanche rescue. Their use is detailed in Appendix 1.

It is worth noting that a lightweight shovel, a collapsible probe, and a transceiver weigh only 1200 gm.

Solo mountaineers and skiers are most vulnerable to avalanches, as even a partial burial can have dire consequences. Recently a lone, cross-country skier was avalanched above the Chalamain Gap, and although only buried up to the knees, was able to extricate himself only after a long, arduous struggle.

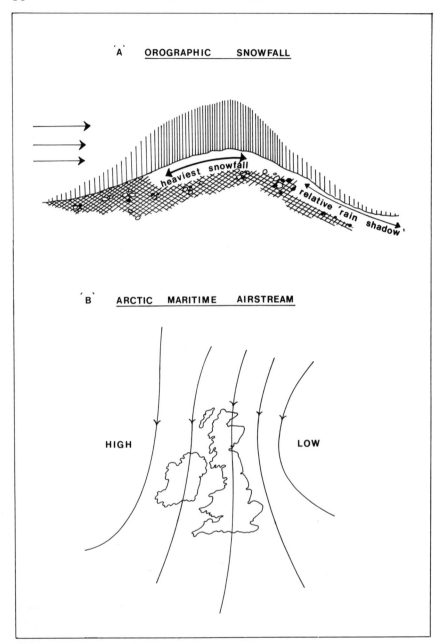

Figure 27

Avalanche awareness should also combine a knowledge of recent weather conditions with general observations on the hill to allow an overall assessment of avalanche risk to be made.

Pre-trip Information

It is usually possible to make a reasonable prediction of snow conditions on the hill, from the patterns of snowfall, wind, and temperature over the previous days or weeks. This can not only alert one to the possibility of avalanches, but allows one to guess where the best climbing or skiing conditions will be found. This weather information is best obtained from day to day observation, but a series of weather maps can provide similar data.

Snowfall

Any heavy snowfall is a likely hazard both in itself and, by overloading existing weak layers in the snowpack. Snowfall at 1000 m is likely to be about twice that recorded at sea-level, because of the orographic lifting of the airstream by the mountain mass, a process which induces precipitation. (Of course, snow precipitated high on the mountain may be drifted to lower levels.) A typical synoptic pattern associated with heavy snowfall in the Scottish mountains involves a cold, northerly airstream of Arctic maritime air, but any moisture-laden wind may bring snow. In the Cairngorms heavy snowfalls are often associated with occluded fronts. The effect of a snowfall must be interpreted in the light of information on wind, and temperature.

Wind

A snowfall in cold, still air would be expected to produce a uniform blanket of powder snow over the hills. This is comparatively rare in Scotland, and it is usual for winds of 20 knots and above to accompany a snowfall.

In these conditions snow is deposited as wind-slab on lee slopes and in sheltered depressions and one can make a prediction of the most likely accumulation zones for a particular direction of snow-bearing wind. Thus a north-east wind would be expected to load slopes in the south-west quadrant with cornices and wind-slab, but it should be understood that this is only a first approximation, and that the ever-changing air-flow over complex mountain terrain can deposit isolated pockets of wind-slab even on windward slopes.

Temperature

A major thaw occurs when the freezing level is above the mountain tops. This is aggravated by warm winds and rainfall. In Britain the sun is a serious melting influence only in the spring, or on snow next to areas of bare rock.

During a thaw, free water is released in the snow, and this can destroy the cohesion of the snowpack and the strength of its anchors. A heavy thaw indicates a danger both of wet, loose snow and of wet slab avalanches, together with a risk of cornice collapse. In these conditions, climbing and off-piste skiing are likely to be unpleasant in wet, heavy "porridge". However, a freeze following the thaw produces a very hard, strong snowpack. If the freeze penetrates to ground level, any avalanche activity is very unlikely, and the hard snow produced is ideal for climbing, though rather too icy for comfortable skiing.

If temperatures are below zero, in normal, windy conditions any fresh snowfall will be deposited as wind-slab, but also, any existing snowpack that has not been stabilised by freeze–thaw can be eroded, transported and re-deposited elsewhere as wind-slab. This is a serious source of dangerous wind-slab in Scotland, and one that shows the limitations of the **"24-hour rule"** (see Chapter I, p. 7) since it is clear that this type of deposition has little direct connection with the timing of the initial snowfall.

At sub-zero temperatures *ET met* is the main stabilising influence on the snowpack, but at low temperatures (below $-10°$) the metamorphism proceeds very slowly and wind-slab or powder snow can remain unstable for long periods.

Many of the worst avalanches in Scotland have followed a week or more of consistently cold weather with snow showers or drifting. **These conditions should be regarded as a powerful indicator of potential avalanche danger.**

In winter the air temperature usually drops about 1°C for every

200 metres ascended, and so Ben Nevis summit at 1343 m is likely to be 7–8° colder than Fort William at sea level.

A knowledge of recent weather patterns can allow one to choose the best area for climbing or skiing. For instance, much of the winter of 1979 saw deep powder snow ideal for skiing in the Cairngorms, but good climbing conditions of hard snow in the lower, warmer regions of the North-west Highlands and Skye that had been subjected to a cycle of melting and re-freezing. The following table indicates the type of deductions that can be made.

Typical pattern of winter weather in Scotland.

Day	Precipitation at 1000 m	Wind at 1000 m	Temperature at 1000 m	Snow conditions at 1000 m
Mon.	None	W 25 kt	+5°C	Heavy thaw. Danger of wet
Tues.	Heavy rain	SW 40 kt	+4°C	snow avalanches and collapsing cornices.
Wed.	None	N 15 kt	−8°C	Hard frost. No avalanche danger. Hard icy snow. Good climbing conditions. Difficult hard snow for skiing.
Thur.	Heavy snow showers	N 30 kt	−6°C	Extensive drifting. Wind-slab and cornices forming,
Fri.	Persistent snow	N 50 kt	−6°C	especially on south-facing slopes. Blizzard conditions.
Sat.	None	Light, variable	−12°C	Low temperatures mean that
Sun.	None	NE 10 kt	−9°C	avalanche danger persists on south-facing slopes.
Mon.	None	SE 30 kt	−6°C	Change of wind direction and continued low temperatures indicate widespread erosion on south slopes and considerable drifting and build-up of wind-slab on NW slopes. Continuing avalanche risk on all slopes.

Note that sea-level weather data, as usually supplied in newspapers and radio weather reports must be corrected for use at 1000 metres by these factors:

Snowfall at 1000 m is about 2 times that at sea-level.
Windspeed at 1000 m is about 2–3 times that at sea-level.
Temperature at 1000 m is about 5°C lower than at sea-level.

General Observations in the Field

An awareness of changing snow-types and weather during a journey in the hills can both enhance one's enjoyment and provide a basis for the evaluation of avalanche danger.

Temperature

The term "temperature" is used imprecisely in skiing and mountaineering because the point of measurement is rarely specified. A temperature measured a standard 1·25 metres above the snow surface can be very different from that measured at the snow surface, which in turn differs from that measured some distance below the snow surface.

Subjective judgements of temperature can be even more misleading—a winter anticyclone can give sunny weather with very hard frosts, but this can *feel* much warmer than a strong rain or sleet-bearing wind that is actually melting snow.

The most important decision to make is whether or not the snowpack is melting. There are various pointers to this:

Thaw conditions	Freezing conditions
Free water in snowpack	No free water
Drips can be squeezed from snowball	No drips
Black bare patches appear on rocks	Bare patches on rocks are dry or ice glazed
Boots get wet	Boots stay fairly dry
Icicles drip	No drips
Streams low on the mountain become swollen	Streams and trickles of water freeze or subside

When a large change of temperature occurs, it takes some time for the change to penetrate the whole snowpack so, for instance, the upper 20 cm can be hard frozen above a base of wet snow.

In thaw conditions wet snow avalanches and collapsing cornices are possible and it is wise to avoid steep slopes and corniced gullies. The heavier the thaw, the more dangerous are snow conditions likely to be.

Fortunately these conditions are not too difficult to recognise, and it is not uncommon for wet snow avalanches to give some degree of warning. Thus wet loose snow avalanches can be preceded by smaller sloughs and the very large wet slab avalanches, such as the regular spring slide in Coire an Lochain in the Cairngorms, are usually heralded by the appearance of impressive crevasses and bergschrunds.

A thaw is particularly dangerous when any kind of snowslab lies on smooth rock slabs or long grass. These can become excellent sliding surfaces when lubricated by melt-water.

In very cold, still conditions, atmospheric water vapour can freeze onto the snow surface as brittle plates of surface hoar. (Hoar forms from water vapour, rime from tiny liquid water droplets.) These crystals are very beautiful, but can be very dangerous if they survive for long enough to provide a fragile foundation for a subsequent snowfall. This is most likely on sheltered northerly slopes, where the sun cannot destroy the surface hoar.

SURFACE HOAR

Figure 28

In cold conditions, wind-slab is the main hazard, and an observation of wind and snowfall is necessary.

Wind and Snowfall

It is important to observe local wind speed and direction, and to note any new or continuing build-up of wind-slab. Erosion features such as *sastrugi* or raised footprints, and deposition features such as cornices or drifts behind boulders are all pointers to the development of wind-slab on lee slopes.

Any blowing spindrift is direct evidence of drifting, but it is easy to underestimate its degree. If the actual rate of build-up of a wind-slab can be observed this can quantify the intensity of precipitation. An increase of slab depth of 5 cm/hour is to be considered dangerously high.

A clue to recent wind-direction can be gained from fresh deposits of rime-ice on rocks, which always form on the windward side.

Any cracks appearing across a slope of wind-slab are likely to be danger signs, and hollow sounding hard snow slopes are likely to be hard-slab over an air gap. Sometimes a section of the upper slab will collapse to provide a timely warning. . . .

If a heavy snowfall occurs with light winds, powder snow avalanches are a possibility. These are usually small and relatively harmless, but certain gullies and depressions can concentrate them with great effect. Zero Gully on Ben Nevis is notorious for this funnelling effect, and several struggling leaders have been plucked from the narrow bottom section of the climb when routine spindrift has suddenly and inexorably built up into an intense stream of powder snow.

The component parts of a snow storm should be noted. A preponderance of needles can lead to compact unstable slabs, or a shower of *graupel* at the passage of a cold front may become the weak layer on which an avalanche runs days or weeks later.

The Suspect Slope

If general observations indicate a possibility of avalanche activity, then a more detailed examination of a particular snowslope should be made. The most effective technique for the climber or skier is the

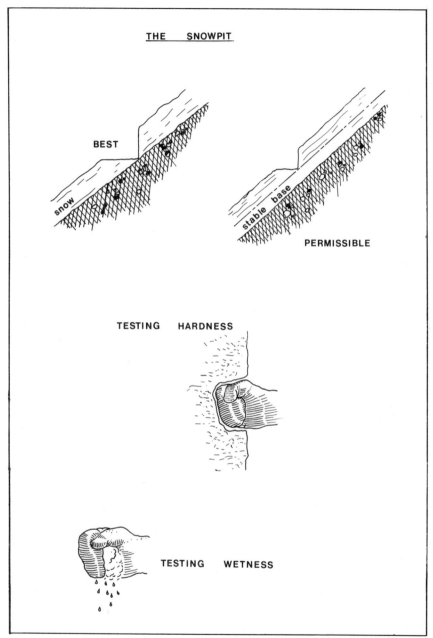

Figure 29

investigation of a snowpit, which is particularly valuable for detecting the threat of slab avalanches.

The Snowpit

The snowpit is dug to expose the stratification of the snowpack. It should be excavated using a shovel, an ice axe or the heel of a ski, to leave a vertical back wall. Ideally it should be dug down to the ground surface, but this can be both strenuous and time consuming. In Scotland an investigation limited to the upper layers will in fact reveal most situations where a slab avalanche threatens.

For maximum information, the pit should be dug at the suspected starting zone of an avalanche, but in practice it is rarely wise to do this on a potentially dangerous slope! Instead the pit is dug at a protected location to the edge of the main avalanche path or one sheltered by a rock outcrop. Much digging will be saved if a relatively shallow part of the snowpack is chosen.

The assumption made is that the stratification seen in the pit will show the same major features as that which would be found at the avalanche starting zone. The closer together that the two sites are, then the more valid this assumption will be. It is also assumed that there are likely to be considerable similarities between different slopes of the same aspect and altitude so that all east-facing slopes at 1000 m would normally display similar snow profiles.

The pit will indicate the likely sequence of layers at the starting zone, but will give no information about the relative depths of these layers, or indeed the total snow depth.

If a cornice and scarp-slope are present near the top of a slope, a snowpit below this level will give no indication of their existence. This is a particular risk in poor visibility when a dangerous scarp-slope can be discovered when one is already fully committed to the climb.

Examination of the Snowpit

The back wall of the pit is brushed clean with a woollen glove or hat, and investigated for different layers. A pencil or the edge of a compass is useful for the gentle probing and scraping which reveals

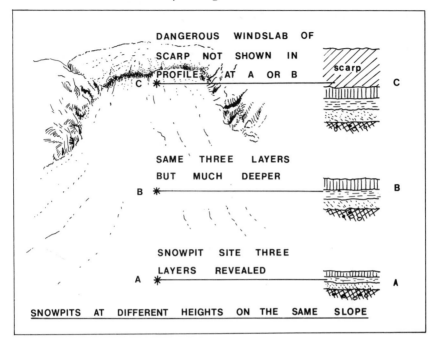

DANGEROUS WINDSLAB OF
SCARP NOT SHOWN IN
PROFILE AT A OR B

scarp

C   C

SAME THREE LAYERS
BUT MUCH DEEPER

B   B

SNOWPIT SITE THREE
LAYERS REVEALED

A   A

<u>SNOWPITS AT DIFFERENT HEIGHTS ON THE SAME SLOPE</u>

Figure 30

thin icy layers. The magnifying lens on a compass can be used to examine snow grains more closely. The physical properties of each layer are assessed and graded as follows:

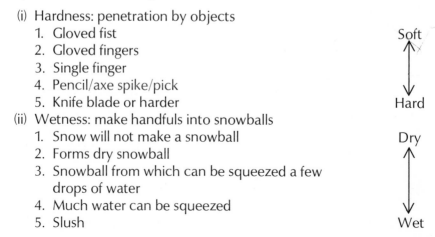

(i) Hardness: penetration by objects
    1. Gloved fist   Soft
    2. Gloved fingers
    3. Single finger
    4. Pencil/axe spike/pick
    5. Knife blade or harder   Hard
(ii) Wetness: make handfuls into snowballs
    1. Snow will not make a snowball   Dry
    2. Forms dry snowball
    3. Snowball from which can be squeezed a few
        drops of water
    4. Much water can be squeezed
    5. Slush   Wet

(iii) Crystal size and nature
    1. Homogenous or less than 1 mm
    2. Less than 2 mm
    3. Less than 3 mm
    4. Less than 4 mm
    5. More than 4 mm

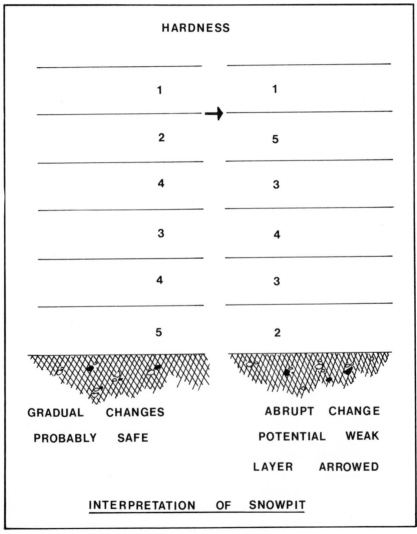

Figure 31

These scales do not allow an accurate quantification of the physical properties of the snowpack, but they aid interpretation of a complex situation. If adjacent layers are very different in physical properties, it is likely that there is a poor adhesion between them. Thus, **any abrupt change in any of the above criteria indicates a potential weak layer**.

In examining the snow profile, particular notice should be taken of spaces between layers, layers of loose, unbonded crystals and of icy crusts, as these often occur at the bed surface of a slab avalanche.

After careful examination of the profile, a section of the slab above it can be isolated. The force necessary to break this test slab from its anchors gives an idea of the strength of any weak layers. In critical situations the test slab may break away under its own weight; in very stable conditions it is necessary to jump on the slab to dislodge it.

Sometimes a slab will consistently fracture at a particular level in

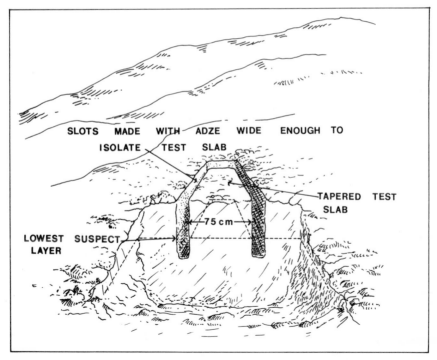

SLOTS MADE WITH ADZE WIDE ENOUGH TO ISOLATE TEST SLAB

TAPERED TEST SLAB

←75 cm→

LOWEST SUSPECT LAYER

Figure 32

an apparently homogenous section of the snowpack. These weaknesses may correspond to a change in the pattern of the storm that deposited the snow.

If the upper layers of the snowpack are found to be loose, incohesive snow either as powder snow, or very wet snow, then loose snow avalanches are more likely than slab avalanches.

Technical Investigations

It is possible to make a much more detailed investigation of the snowpack, using ram penetrometers, shear frames and the like. In the Alps a wide and systematic investigation is made in this way, and used for national avalanche prediction, but it is unlikely that such a scheme will develop in Scotland. Isolated penetrometer profiles are of interest but are difficult to interpret and inconvenient to obtain. We will not cover the subject here, but excellent accounts are to be found in the "Avalanche Handbook" and "Avalanches & Snow Safety" (see Appendix 4, p. 111).

Assessing the Risk

An attempt should be made to rate the slope as: Safe

Marginal

Unsafe

If no weak layers or unusual influences are present, the slope should be safe. No further investigation is necessary. If some risk of avalanche is recognised, the degree of the risk can be assessed by referring to various other criteria.

Depth of Snow

Thick, heavy layers of wind-slab produce a much greater shearing force on any weak layer than would a shallow wind-slab. On an open slope, a slab 5–10 cm in depth is not normally considered a serious hazard, but any funnelling of the snow, or any local increase in thickness, could make it so. These local variations of slab depth are easily missed in conditions of bad visibility.

Terrain and Route to be Followed

Steeper slopes are more likely to fracture than gentler ones of the same structure. The range of 30–45° are the common slope angles for large slab avalanches. There seem to be no upper limits of angles for avalanches in Scottish gullies. The channelling or funnelling effect in a gully will also greatly amplify the force of an avalanche.

Slope profile also comes into consideration when a party is faced unavoidably with crossing a convex slope. Generally speaking, it is better to cross high up, so as to be near the top of any potential avalanche. This leaves the possibility of escape upwards and also means that burial may be much less deep. Against this, it is wise to avoid the zones of tension which exist on convexities. In areas such as the Cairngorms, where convex slopes abound, the decision as to where to cross can thus be a fine one. If the choice exists, direct descent is always preferable to traversing, as the horizontal weaknesses produced by traversing may more easily propagate a *crown-wall* fracture.

If avalanche conditions prevail, the climber is wise to avoid steep, open slopes and gullies and to stick to ridges and buttresses.

Type of Snow

A small avalanche of fluffy powder snow will be much less destructive than one of concrete-like wet snow. The intact blocks of a hard slab avalanche can be much more damaging than soft slab, where the blocks soon break up as they slide.

The very largest slab avalanches are usually of hard slab, since only a hard, rigid material is able to propagate fractures over long distances.

High Risk Situations

A number of further considerations arise when one is faced unavoidably with crossing a dangerous slope. This may occur at the end of a long day, when the only alternatives seem more risky, or at other times in serious mountaineering situations, such as in the greater ranges or on rescues. These are presented as points to think about, rather than as specific precautions, since circumstances will dictate the precise course of action.

One at a Time

There is no point in exposing the whole party to avalanche risk simultaneously. The members who are awaiting their turn, or who have already crossed or descended should stand in a safe place, observing the progress of the person currently negotiating the slope. It is worth remembering that an avalanche may occur even after several persons have already crossed the slope.

In blizzard conditions with zero visibility, the necessity for keeping the party together may over-rule this advice.

Belaying

If the dangerous slope is a small one (e.g. a narrow gully which must be crossed), it may be possible to belay party members individually with a rope. There is a possibility that a person held by a rope in this way may be injured by the crushing action of large masses of avalanche snow, but this disadvantage should be weighed against the possibility of being swept over cliffs or into other hazardous situations. Belaying will be impracticable on a long open slope, but it may then be possible to link up islands of safety, such as groups of large boulders.

Clothing

To prevent blocking of the mouth and nasal passages with snow, it seems wise to cover the face with a scarf or tightly fastened anorak hood. Also, a warmly clothed victim has a better chance of survival, as many avalanche casualties die of hypothermia, or a combination of this with asphyxia.

Procedure with Skis

In some snow conditions a ski will have a much greater cutting effect than would a traverse on foot, whilst in others, the skis will prevent the mountaineer from cutting a dangerously deep trough, but in general it is wise to remove the skis, since they are a serious encumbrance if an avalanche does occur. The feeling of security in speed that skis offer is largely an illusion, and whilst accomplished skiers have skied out of avalanches, many more cases exist where skis and sticks have dragged the wearer further down into the debris. Try getting up from a fall in deep powder snow and then imagine what it would be like if the whole slope were proceeding downhill with irresistible acceleration.

Finally, it must be stressed that all these "precautions" are a very poor substitute for avoiding the dangerous slope altogether.

Survival Action if Caught

The fate of a person caught in an avalanche will largely be a matter of luck, but there may be the possibility of some defensive action. Improvisation on the following themes has sometimes been of help.

Delaying Departure

Driving an ice-axe or other implement into the sub-strata may prevent the climber being swept away if the avalanche is a small one. Even if this only delays departure for a few seconds it will have the beneficial effect of helping to ensure that the victim is deposited nearer the top of the avalanche where burial is likely to be less deep. If near the fracture line of a slab avalanche, a convulsive leap up-slope may land you on safe ground above the wall.

Getting Rid of Gear

It is probably wise to loosen rucksack waist straps and/or remove ski safety straps to lessen the possibility of being impeded or injured by these items. On the other hand, victims have sometimes been rescued due to a protruding ski tip.

A Quick Look Round

Before departure and while falling, it is often possible to take a look round to see where you are in relation to safe ground. This may enable you to run or roll off to the side. Rolling like a log is quite an effective technique as it maximises the chance of staying on the surface.

Shouting

While falling, shouting may attract the attention of observers to your location.

The Ice-axe

The question is whether to retain or attempt to throw away the axe. Some climbers have been badly injured in avalanches by ice-axes whirling uncontrolled on the end of a wrist loop. In practice, if a sling is in use, it is unlikely that the climber will be able to get it off in an avalanche. If no sling is used and the climber has not dropped the axe in the initial confusion, it is probably worth trying to retain it. At least one climber succeeded in ice-axe braking on the hard sub-stratum, allowing the avalanche to pass over him. However, co-ordinated movement underneath a moving avalanche is difficult, even in powder.

Riding it Down

If a victim is fortunate enough to be on the surface, efforts should be made to remain there. Swimming motions may help; the writer can recommend backstroke. In a hard slab avalanche, try to remain on top of a block, thus sledging down. Several amazing escapes are attributable to this method.

The Terminal Stages

As the avalanche comes to a halt make a huge effort to stay on the surface or to at least thrust a hand out of the snow. Many people have been rescued due to a protruding hand or finger. The other hand is probably best employed in covering the mouth and nose and in trying to preserve airspace round the face.

Most authorities advise the buried victim not to panic. This may be difficult, but unproductive shouting or struggling will only use up more air. It is unlikely that all the members of the party will have been buried and help will probably be at hand.

In summary, these methods may not ensure survival, but many of them have been of value to parties in the past. Some of them are mutually exclusive, but circumstanc :s will dictate which are feasible.

Avalanche Rescue

Self-rescue

Sometimes people are able to dig themselves out after burial by an avalanche. They are more likely to succeed in this if they manage to avoid panic, and are unhampered by rucksacks, skis and ski sticks.

Rescue by Companions

The witness or survivor of an avalanche has undergone a shocking and disorientating experience, yet it is his capacity for clear thought

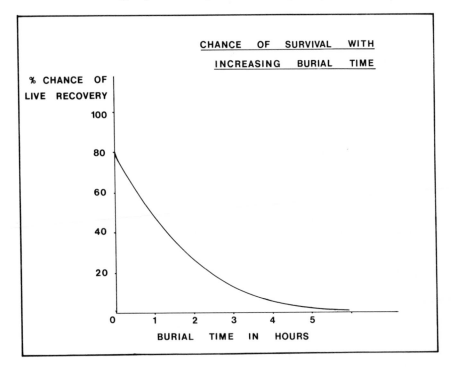

Figure 33

and speedy, efficient action that will maximise the chances of survival of his buried companions.

An analysis of many Alpine avalanche accidents gives the graph (fig. 33), which indicates that after 2 hours only 20% of completely buried victims are recovered alive. This makes it clear that the companions of the buried members of the party, working **immediately** with limited resources have a greater chance of making a successful rescue than a well equipped rescue team arriving some hours later. It should be noted however that a small chance of live recovery remains even after several day's burial.

In the light of these and other statistics it is possible to suggest the strategy that is likely to give maximum success.

Check for Further Danger

Sometimes, particularly in branched gully systems, one avalanche may trigger off another. A brief check that another avalanche is not imminent is worthwhile.

Mark Last Seen Point

Marking the point at which a victim was struck by the avalanche, and the point where he was last seen moving with the debris, will help to define his path down the slope. A line through these points and continuing down the flow-line of the avalanche can be estimated and marked, and there is a good chance that the victim will lie close to this line.

The points should be physically marked with ski-sticks or rucksacks, as merely fixing the position by eye is unreliable. This can be difficult and it may be best for one person to keep his eye on the spot to be marked while directing another where to place the marker.

Quick Search

The party should make a quick search of the debris looking for obvious signs of a buried person, and listening carefully for calls or whistles. This search is of **vital** importance—lives have often been

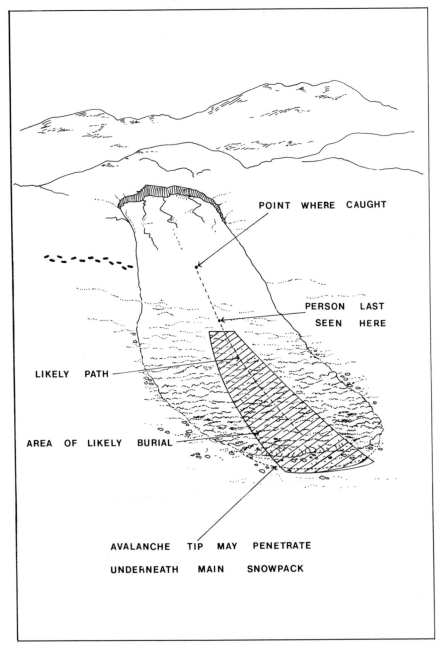

POINT WHERE CAUGHT

PERSON LAST
SEEN HERE

LIKELY PATH

AREA OF LIKELY BURIAL

AVALANCHE TIP MAY PENETRATE
UNDERNEATH MAIN SNOWPACK

Figure 34

lost when shocked survivors have gone for help, leaving an easily located victim partially buried but unable to breathe.

Thorough Search

If the quick search fails to recover all the victims, the party must make a more thorough search, paying particular attention to the avalanche tip and to any points where debris can pile up against ledges, boulders, or other obstacles. Probing with axes, ski sticks or collapsible probes, should be systematic and well organised. A coarse probe on a grid of about 70 cm is probably best. Alpine statistics indicate that the average buried depth is about 1·4 m, so improvised probing with axes is of much less value than that with longer probes. (However, most live rescues occur from a depth of 1 m or less.)

A party equipped with transceivers and practised in their use has a much better chance of locating a buried companion than one without these aids. It is wise to follow the instructions of the manufacturer in using these instruments, but normally the search consists of two phases: (1) long range location when the party sweep the slope in order to detect the signal from the victim, and (2) short range location when the position of the victim can be pinpointed to an accuracy of about one third of the depth of burial. These techniques are detailed in Appendix 1.

Transceivers exist in a confusing range of frequencies, and there would be much value in the universal adoption of the UIAA recommended standard frequency of 2·275 kHz (as in Skadi & Pieps 2). (Sets such as Pieps 3 and Ortovox function both on 2·275 kHz and on the frequency of 457 kHz which is widely used in the Swiss Barryvox [Autophon] system.)

Send for Help

If the party is fairly large one or two people can be sent for help by a safe route, while the rest of the party continue the search. The previously mentioned survival times indicate that, unless he is unusually close to help, a solitary witness is probably best advised to search for at least one or two hours before leaving the scene to enlist assistance.

> **Check Further Danger**
> **Mark Last Seen Point**
> **QUICK SEARCH!!**
> **Thorough Search**
> **Send for Help**

When the victim is located he should be dug out at once. A portable shovel is about 5 times as effective as an ice-axe or the heel of a ski. As soon as the victim's head is exposed resuscitation or the supply of warm drinks should be commenced. The person who has been buried may be severely hypothermic and may have no apparent signs of life.

Organised Avalanche Rescue

Avalanche Dogs

Trained avalanche dogs are highly effective in locating buried persons, and in good condition they can search an area in perhaps one tenth the time that a team of 20 men equipped with probes would take.

Compact, non-porous, icy snow will limit the passage of the scent of the victim, and make the use of dogs less effective, as will the presence of distracting scents and severe weather.

Trained dogs will always be used with their handler, and usually work from down-wind. If a dog is immediately available it is wise to keep other rescuers off the avalanche debris, and to discourage them from urination near the site, so as not to confuse the dog, although "resting" the slope for 10 minutes after searchers have operated will allow many of the false scents to dissipate. In any case, the vital search by people on the spot must not be delayed by the expectation of the appearance of a dog.

Typical times for the thorough search of a square of 100 m side (1 hectare) by a well trained dog would be about 30 minutes for a coarse search and 1–2 hours for a fine one, but may be faster. In

Figure 35

Britain, the Search and Rescue Dog Association (SARDA) undertake the provision and training of such dogs and their handlers.

Probing

This is the traditional method of searching for buried persons, and involves the systematic probing of the debris with rigid metal probes of about 3 m in length. It is worth noting that the avalanche tip may drive under the main snowpack. This is most likely with dense, wet snow avalanches and allowance for this should be made in the area searched.

Ideally, each probing team consists of 20 searchers under the direction of a probe-master (much larger teams are very unwieldy). They are backed up by a shovel party, and if necessary a lookout is posted in a safe place to warn of a further avalanche. The searchers should be briefed as to an escape route in the event of further avalanche.

The area to be searched should be marked with coloured flags, and if sufficient manpower is available, two men holding a cord along the line of probes at snow level is useful to keep the line straight. The probe-master's job is to ensure that the probings follow a systematic pattern. Two types of search pattern are normally used:

Coarse Probe

This gives a coarse grid of 70 × 75 cm, which has only a 75% chance of locating a buried person.

The search-line stand elbow to elbow, hands on hips to define the spacing. On the command "Probe" the probe is inserted between the searcher's feet, and pushed down until an obstruction is felt, or until the top of the probe is at about waist height (probing deeper is wasteful of time).

The probe-master checks the line of probes and on the command "Probe" the line extracts the probes, takes one pace forwards and inserts the probes again. This process continues. If a searcher feels he might have found something he leaves his probe in place as a marker and informs the shovel party. They will give the searcher a

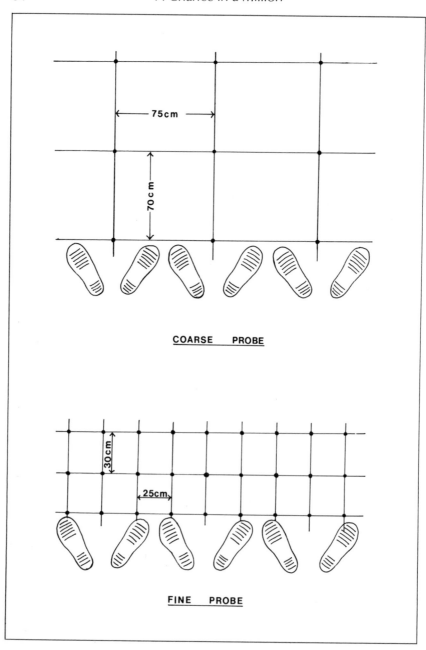

Figure 36

replacement probe and dig at the indicated point. The line must continue to search until a definite location is made by the shovel party.

Fine Probe

This is done by probing at each foot and between the feet, before taking a half step forward. This gives a grid of 25 × 30 cm with a near 100% chance of finding a body.

However, to search an area of 1 hectare, 20 men will require 4 hours for a coarse probe and about 20 hours for a fine probe. This means that the fine probe is so slow that it is not normally used for locating live persons. Two consecutive coarse probes give a better chance of effecting a live rescue than a single fine probe.

Size of grid	Coarse probe	Fine probe
Chance of location (victim at 1·4 m)	75%	100%
Time for 20 men to search 1 hectare	About 4 hours	About 20 hours

Other Methods

Many other methods of locating buried persons have been tried, including radar, metal detectors and heat detectors. None of these has proved to be consistently useful.

IV The Grey Zone

Avalanche incidents and accidents vary in their consequences from the possibly hilarious to the definitely tragic, and there is no way of knowing at the start what the outcome will be. The following short accounts cover this spectrum, but also span a range of perceived avalanche risk, so that in some incidents the danger of avalanche was blatantly obvious to the participants, while at the other extreme, no avalanche danger at all was anticipated. In between comes a body of incidents where the persons avalanched had probably appreciated that a certain level of risk existed, but had decided that this was marginal. It will be seen from the records of these incidents that the consequences of the accidents do not always reflect the degree of caution exercised by the mountaineers concerned. Readers are invited to study these accounts and in the light of their own experience, along with the other contents of this handbook, to decide whether their actions would have differed from those of the avalanche victims.

Ben Nevis, April 1965

The following lines are extracted from a letter sent to Blyth Wright by the late Philip Tranter, one of the most energetic and prolific personalities to bestride the Scottish climbing scene in the Sixties. As the moral to be drawn from the account is obvious, it is offered without further comment. Nevertheless, the reader will deduce from it something of Tranter's overpowering enthusiasm for every aspect of the mountain experience.

"And another thing too, I forgot, Wul and I were avalanched out of No 4 Gully on Nevis on Sunday! Hellish weather, right back in the dead of winter. Rather depressing after the fabulous weather at Carnmore. A vast depth of new snow on old base, perfect avalanche conditions. We set off hoping to try No 2, but soon gave that idea up. Instead waded up to No 4, conferred at foot, saw four avalanches, decided it would be foolish to continue, continued, got 300 ft up gully, me 30 ft ahead. Were duly avalanched, swept down 500 ft. I've heard it said one is supposed to try to swim the stuff, but that was so much rot in that particular avalanche. It took me the whole way down, which seemed ages, just to get a decent effective grip on my axe and start trying to dig it into the hard snow below (I was underneath all the debris).

Movement relative to the snow (old debris itself), was almost impossible. Like trying to play ping-pong in treacle. Wul, poor sod, lost his axe. His hands were pinned behind him and he couldn't breathe. When we stopped and I crawled out I at first thought I was going to have to use my skill at artificial respiration on Wul, but he came round spluttering and cheerful. Funny thing was, I never even felt breathless. Still, it was all good British fun and enlivened an otherwise rather dreary day."

Ben Nevis, April 1, 1967

Many further accidents have occurred on the well-trodden slopes of Coire na Ciste on Ben Nevis. Because of the nature of the terrain, many of them, like Tranter's, have not had serious consequences. However, two years after the lucky escape recounted above, an accident occurred which could well have resulted in the deaths of both victims.

The two climbers involved, Andrew Philipson and his cousin, David Richardson, were both experienced climbers, Philipson being a member of the elite Alpine Climbing Group. Their equipment also appears to have been good and they were very well clad, a fact which later would be of great significance.

Weather conditions were very bad as the pair climbed the steepening ground towards the foot of No 3 Gully, which was their day's objective. It was fairly cold and a strong gusty wind and much new snow made navigation awkward, to the extent that the climbers were unable to find No 3 Gully. They decided that they were too far right and started traversing further rightwards in the hope of finding

No 4 Gully. The slope at this point is fairly steep, about 40° and one wonders whether at this point the two were debating the wisdom of continuing. The risk of avalanche must have been manifest to an experienced party, but no decision to retreat was made.

Events were in any case about to make decisions superfluous, for at about 2 p.m. both men were avalanched, carried along the surface for a few seconds and then covered by the sliding mass. Their fall was later estimated at 160 m and when the avalanche finally ran to a halt, both men were buried. Their plight was desperate; no one had witnessed their fall and although new snow contains much air, asphyxia might easily have been their fate. Barring this, death from exposure frequently overtakes the avalanche victim. By great good fortune, however, both men were able to breathe and both, as previously indicated, were well clad. Richardson, for example, wore a string vest, long woollen underpants, a wool shirt, 3 sweaters, wool breeches, knee-length canvas gaiters, 2 pairs of stockings and a cotton anorak.

Philipson found himself in a hole about four feet beneath the surface, normally not a survivable position. However, the will to live must have been strong, for after nine hours of effort, scraping and scratching at the snow, he emerged almost unhurt into the night air. While no doubt thankful for his own escape, he must have entertained little hope for his friend. Turning his steps downwards, he made for the nearest aid, at the Charles Inglis Clark Hut (CIC), where some Oxford climbers were in residence. Although the hut is close beneath the great cliffs, the way down must have seemed long and, finally to stumble into its warmth, a great release.

The Oxford men in the hut acted with commendable speed and after 'phoning the Police in Fort William, set off to search for Richardson. Following Philipson's tracks back to the avalanche tip, they set to without much hope of success. For one person to survive a nine-hour burial was one thing: to expect another to be alive after 11 hours was too much. Nevertheless, soon after midnight, one searcher saw a hand protruding from the snow. Furious digging revealed a man alive and conscious; Richardson also had escaped.

These remarkable survivals are surpassed only by that of Robert Burnett, recounted in Chapter I. The Oxford climbers almost certainly saved the second victim by their prompt action, for although the

Lochaber team arrived at the same time as the stretcher party arrived back at the CIC Hut, the extra delay might well have been fatal. One could wish that all those who are in a position to do a "first search" after an avalanche would act with similar despatch and effectiveness.

Stob a'Choire Odhair (Blackmount), November 27, 1938

Ben Nevis has no monopoly of avalanche danger and many lesser mountains have caused problems for the mountaineer. The hills along the West Highland Railway from Crianlarich to the Blackmount were popular in the years prior to the Second World War and the pages of the Scottish Mountaineering Club Journal at this time contain several accounts of avalanches. H. MacRobert in his 1938 article, "Ski-Running", mentions an incident near Cruach Ardrain, where his companion on skis was knocked over by a small wind-slab avalanche. This was dislodged by MacRobert's skis and completely buried his friend, who was about 30 m below him. This is the earliest Scottish incident involving skiers of which the present writers have knowledge.

In the same article, MacRobert mentions "the enormous wet-snow avalanche on Ben More which carried away one of our members and spread out fan-wise over about 10,000 square yards to a depth of over 10 feet". The member involved was obviously lucky to escape as the mass of snow released on the figures given would be about 15,000 tonnes.

It is unusual in such early accounts to have any observational data, even such as the estimates of size given in the Ben More incident. However, the following event, also recorded in the 1938 Scottish Mountaineering Club Journal, is exceptional in the detail given: it is also noteworthy as being still one of the few November incidents on record:

'Traversing a broad ledge on snow at 45°, a large section suddenly avalanched and both men were carried down 300–400 feet. The snow was soft and about 2 feet deep. Rain had been falling for some time and something like a storm was still in progress. The top 4–5 inches of the snow was saturated and granular and was packing down under the action of wind and rain. Below the snow was powdery.

"It would appear that the avalanche was caused by the top layer sliding off from the powder snow due to the lateral cutting disturbance made by the traverse. The debris was over 100 feet wide and mostly about 4 feet in depth."

The persons involved in this incident were J. R. Wood and A. C. D. Small, of whom Small was injured in the avalanche but was able to descend unaided.

Even at this distance in time it is possible, from the detailed information given, to see the main factors producing the avalanche; a poor bond between the underlying layers of different crystalline type and size, along with overloading due to the saturation of the surface layer. The mountaineers concerned obviously had a good understanding of the factors governing avalanche release and yet had elected to cross the slope. At that time a snowpit examination of the slope was not normal practice and the conventional view was that Scottish snow was "not much prone to avalanche". Applying modern knowledge and technique, would this incident have been avoided? The only answer is a definite "Maybe".

Ben Lui, May 12, 1934

The shapely and isolated peak of Ben Lui is another of those accessible from the West Highland Railway, standing to the south of the line between Crianlarich and Tyndrum. Its Central Gully, a fine natural line leading directly to the summit, has long been one of the classic snow climbs of Scotland. Seen face on, it still looks fully steep enough to daunt or to inspire the aspirant snow and ice climber. The mountain is nowadays known as the site of several avalanche incidents, including one which in a February blizzard of 1957, carried down four members of an RAF Mountain Rescue Team, resulting in a broken leg for one of the unfortunate climbers.

However, the earliest full account of an avalanche in the Central Gully has been left to us by the late Ben Humble, a man whose life would in itself merit a weighty volume. The part which he played in the establishment of the Mountain Rescue service in Scotland is, perhaps, less well-known than it ought to be. However, his contribution to the literature and photography of Scottish mountains speaks its own story, while his idiosyncratic approach to the hills has been immortalised by abler pens than ours. Ben was an active climber in his younger days and his enthusiasm led him on one occasion, with three companions, to the Central Gully of Ben Lui. The following account is largely a paraphrase of Ben's words.

As the party approached the foot of the Gully that morning, they noted much avalanche debris, but once established on the climb, found very fine conditions. It is interesting that from this point there is no further mention of possible avalanche contained in Ben's account. They made good progress towards the large cornice which defended the summit. This obstacle was overcome by digging a six-foot tunnel and the climbers reached the summit in brilliant sunshine.

At 2.30 p.m. the descent was begun and as they intended to return by the route of ascent the party roped up meaning to unrope when the summit snowfield had been negotiated and the top of the Gully proper had been reached. They would then unrope and glissade down singly.

All four climbers were strung out on the upper snowfield, with the last man immediately below the cornice when, starting just below the last man, the whole upper snowfield started to avalanche and all were carried away.

The lowest man on the slope saw that the slide would carry him not into the Gully, but over the rocks to its side. He made a jump and landed on snow which was pouring towards the Gully. All the others followed. The snow piled up many feet deep, filling up the Gully and tumbling the first two climbers over at great speed. The last two men on the rope succeeded in remaining feet first and on top of the avalanche. Finally, after 500 m of helpless descent, the men found themselves lying amongst the debris, well below the start of the Central Gully.

Thankfully, the climbers gathered their wits and their pieces of equipment. As the slope at this point was gentle, they unroped prior to completing their descent. However, the price for their morning's climb was not yet fully paid. As they stood impotently on the slope,

D

another avalanche broke off from the upper west snowfield and hurtled towards them. Were they to be engulfed by this new peril? The answer, it seemed, was in the negative and they had a moment of relief as the second avalanche ran to a halt a short distance above them.

As it happened, one member of the party had gone back up the slope into the lee of a large rock in order to retrieve a lost ice-axe and so was spared what happened next. The detail of what occurred is uncertain, as accounts are understandably confused, but it seems that the shock of the second avalanche started the original avalanche tip moving again. In any event, the result was that the three remaining members of the party were carried down another 70 m or so; again, unbelievably unhurt, after a total descent bordering on 550 m. This is still the record for a Scottish avalanche and May 12 remains as the latest date in the year on which a party has been carried down by an avalanche.

Unfortunately for our purposes, Ben has not left in his account any indication as to the type of avalanche which figured in this incident. It would be easy to assume that because of the strong sunshine and the time of the year, melting of the upper layers of the snowpeak was responsible for the avalanches. However, this tempting extrapolation would be based on insufficient evidence. Wintry weather and accumulation of wind-slab in May are by no means uncommon and bright sunshine, even then, does not guarantee high temperatures. Nevertheless, the wet-snow avalanche theory remains by far the most likely.

As a footnote, the total damage in this remarkable incident was one lost ice-axe and one rucksack missing. The latter item turned up a month later when the snow had melted. It contained a camera with an exposed film which developed perfectly, providing the participants in this event with a pictorial record of their day, which however was unlikely to be as vivid as the cerebral images they retained.

Cairngorm—Ben MacDui Plateau, December 8, 1976

Undoubtedly, knowledge and forethought can greatly reduce the chance of being caught in an avalanche. Nevertheless, it is as well to admit that there are some cases in which marginal risk is perceived, when even a careful examination of the snowpack, combined with a long experience of the winter hills, will not adequately protect the party. The following incidents emphasise this point.

The early winter of 1976 brought fairly heavy snowfalls to the Cairngorms, but by early December, a period of fine, cold weather had set in. For 10 days or so, clear skies greeted lucky mountaineers, although fairly strong winds caused a considerable build-up of new slab in sheltered locations, lying on a pre-existing base of hard névé. Nevertheless, the 10 days from the end of November were without new snowfall.

Glenmore Lodge parties set out on the mornings of both December 7 and 8, in order to bivouac in snow shelters at two different locations. On the 7th, Martin Burrows-Smith set out to spend two nights at the Garbh Uisge Beag with an experienced group of Winter Mountain Leader Assessment candidates, while on the 8th, Blyth Wright took a less experienced party of winter hill-walkers to a much less remote site at Ciste Mhearadh on Cairngorm for a one-night snowhole.

"Obviously there was a risk of avalanche from the new slab lying on old névé and on arrival at Ciste Mhearadh, it was indeed apparent that some feet of slab lay on our proposed site, a steep bank of snow about 10 m high. I immediately set to work probing the slope with an avalanche probe, finding that there was a uniform resistance to penetration throughout the whole depth of the new slab, indicating a homogeneous layer of slab lying on the old névé. This slab was some 2 m thick and in consultation with another instructor who was present, I agreed that the profile of the slope was such that an avalanche of the new slab on the old névé was most unlikely. In this at least we were to be proven correct.

"After having dug some $1\frac{1}{2}$ m into the slope, I was feeling satisfied with the progress of my own snow dwelling, when a shout caused me to stand up. Outside it was all avalanching, and suddenly, irresistibly, I was being propelled down-slope. Fortunately, I was on my back and able to keep on the surface, although the presence of large blocks made burial a real possibility. Then, amazingly, I had stopped, not hurt, able to stand up. Someone was shouting though. One person was missing, buried. Frantic digging revealed the top of a head, then a face, thankfully still breathing. Total injuries, eventually nil, but pride was somewhat ruffled."

This incident caused the instructors concerned some heart-searching, which was not necessarily relieved on arrival at the Lodge to find out that the other Lodge snowhole group had been avalanched not once, but twice. One of these incidents had been at night, when the party was swept 120 m in total darkness above their snowhole sites in Garbh Uisge Beag.

Subsequent investigations at the sites of these incidents showed that little or nothing could have been done to predict them by direct examination of the snowpack. The avalanches had run on a buried layer of surface hoar, which although visible once the avalanche had occurred, is generally agreed to be virtually invisible in the snowpack.

On December 1–4, surface hoar had been visible at Glenmore Lodge, but had not been generally observed on the hill. Similar but different conditions occurred in winter 1982–83 when the Lodge issued an avalanche warning on the basis of extremely severe avalanche conditions due to buried surface hoar at low level, only to find that high-level locations were virtually risk-free.

Cairn Lochain, March 10, 1965

Coire an Lochain has already been singled out in these pages as the birthplace of great avalanches.

Most such avalanches occur in the back of the corrie, in the vicinity of the Great Slab or to the west of it, sometimes filling the whole floor of the Coire with debris metres in depth, smashing the thick ice in the Lochan and carrying blocks of ice to within 200 m of Jean's Hut.

Occasionally, however, the east-facing slope on the western ridge of the Coire can carry dangerous accumulations, particularly when south-west winds cause a great depth of wind-slab to gather. Such a time was March 10, 1965, when a party was descending from the plateau by this slope whose mean angle is only 28°, with a maximum near the top of 35°.

The party was a large one of eight persons, led by two very experienced winter mountaineers. One of these led the way down the slope, with the party following more or less in line. Without warning the firm snow in which they were descending broke away in a huge avalanche the whole width of the slope. The blocks of debris were very large, for this was a hard slab avalanche, with the attendant risk of severe injury due to crushing.

All the ingredients for a tragedy were present, but luck was with this party. Firstly, only three members were carried down, the fracture occurring between the third and fourth members and leaving the others above the *crownwall*. Secondly, all those avalanched were near the fracture line and so near the top of the avalanche. Thirdly, and quite amazingly, all of those carried away succeeded in remaining on top of individual blocks of debris until the very last stages of their terrifying 200 m descent. Other cases are known of similar toboggan rides, but the writers know of no other case where three persons were permitted to escape by this method. In fact, as the avalanche slowed down, one person did become involved with the tumbling blocks and received crushing and bruising injuries, but was able to walk painfully home.

The mass of snow which avalanched on this occasion was about 9,000 tonnes, the maximum width of the slide path being 400 m. Obviously cool heads played a part in the escape of this party, but without the vital element of luck, none would have survived.

Lairig Ghru, March 30, 1975

In examining the records of avalanche incidents, along with the whole of the related meteorological information, it often comes to mind that, had this information been carefully considered by the parties concerned, they might have acted differently. An example is given in Chapter II, p. 51, "A Case History", of the way in which a weather forecast for a mountain area can be used in assessing avalanche risk. It is clear that hill-goers do not always do this.

The end of March 1975 was a period of widespread snow instability in the Cairngorms, as evidenced by the small epidemic of incidents and accidents on the 30th and 31st. The following was the most serious of these and took place a little more than one kilometre from Coire an Lochain, where steep slopes fall westwards to the Lairig Ghru. This famous Cairngorm pass has featured in many a drama over the centuries and it is a place of gloomy reputation. Its slopes between the March Burn and the cliffs of Lurcher's Crag offer relatively easy routes to and from the plateau. Although set at an angle of 35–40° and bouldery, they do not normally constitute dangerous terrain for experienced and competent persons.

The party which set out on that fine morning from Corrour Bothy at the south end of the Lairig, was certainly a competent one. As to experience, they comprised some of the more practised ski-mountaineers in Scotland. On the second day of their ski tour, enjoying the much improved weather, what had they to fear as they climbed on foot up these slopes? Certainly, as one member of the party subsequently wrote, "there was no mention, or as I believe, even thought of avalanche", yet they were about to be involved in the most serious avalanche accident yet to affect a skiing party in Scotland.

The details of what occurred as the party climbed out of the Lairig have been well documented elsewhere (Scottish Mountaineering Club Journal, Vol. XXI, No. 168) but the bare facts are as follows: the party were avalanched near the top of the slope, something under a kilometre north-west of the March Burn. Seven persons were carried down about 200 m. Four members of the party were more or less seriously injured, including back and pelvic injuries, a compound broken arm and serious lacerations. The uninjured survivors reacted quickly in summoning help and within three hours of the accident, the casualties were evacuated by helicopter. As a helicopter had already been scrambled in order to deal with the Coire an Lochain accident (see Chapter II, p. 51), it was possible to divert this aircraft and so expedite the rescue.

One might ask how such an experienced party could meet with an accident like this, particularly in view of the weather history and snow profile discussed in Chapter II, p. 51 ("A Case History"). They might reasonably not have expected slab of the depth which occurred, although some slab build-up could have been anticipated. The slope which avalanched, a shallow gully rather than an open slope, was 4–5 m deep, for that was the height of the *crownwall*. This might have made snowpit observation difficult, if it had been envisaged. A complicating circumstance was that the slope was reportedly covered in *sastrugi*, which is normally taken as a sign that avalanche risk is decreasing. Obviously, however, with a very thick snowpack, the surface layers may exhibit *sastrugi* without the lower layers being affected by the erosion.

It is interesting that one of the party noted a sharp rise in temperature just before the accident happened. It is at least possible in the prevailing conditions of light winds, that as mentioned in Chapter II (p. 57) this was due to a temperature inversion, with the party emerging from a cold into a warm layer. As a matter of record, the temperature at Glenmore Lodge did not rise above $+0.8°C$ all day. To quote once more from Malcolm Smith's Cairngorm Guide, "the fact that they (avalanches and cornice collapses) can occur in conditions of temperature inversion, is less well known".

The action of an inversion as a factor in this incident is only a possibility, but it could have provided the final aggravating factor. The party concerned have been particularly generous in publishing accounts of their experience for the possible benefit of others and the accident was a salutary reminder of what may happen even to a competent party when perhaps their guard has been allowed to fall.

Beinn a'Ghlo, January 14 or 15, 1982

Glen Tilt is an age-old route from Atholl to Deeside in the east, or, in a northerly direction via Glen Feshie or the Lairig Ghru, to Speyside. In much the same way as the Lairig, its length splits a mountain range in two, with high summits on either hand. The best known and highest is Ben a'Ghlo, but there are other worthy goals for the hill-walker and a number of bothies provide basic accommodation. In winter, excellent ski touring is available, but the area does not lack steep slopes which must be treated with care.

These hills, although accessible, are spacious enough for solitary wandering to be enjoyed. Not, however, on January 19 and 20, 1982; on these dates 100 searchers were scouring the hillsides, helicopters flew constantly overhead, civilian, Police and RAF teams along with SARDA rescue dogs combined in a massive operation, in the hope of finding one missing walker.

This man, a doctor, had set out from home on the previous

Thursday, the 13th, and had not arrived back on the Sunday as intended. Although with only the scantiest information as to his plans, the Police found his car on Monday and the huge search was initiated. Weather conditions had been deteriorating over this period, from the fine, cold winter conditions of the week before and Tuesday's search took place in atrocious weather. It was thought that the missing man might have intended going over Beinn a'Ghlo to the remote Tarf bothy and the day's search took place mainly on the slopes of that mountain. It drew a blank.

By now, hope for the missing doctor was at a low ebb. Even if he had been suffering only from some relatively minor injury, his chances of surviving such a prolonged exposure to bad weather, were not good. Nonetheless, Wednesday saw a renewed effort and with better weather, more teams, dogs, and helicopters combed the area.

The day wore on with nothing found when one team from Tayside, searching along the north-west ridge of Beinn a'Ghlo, found some footprints. They were partly melted due to the thaw but were the first possible link with the missing man.

These footprints traversed the side of the hill in a roughly horizontal line. As the search moved along in this direction, the footprints suddenly disappeared. Almost immediately items of equipment were found; a rucksack side pocket, primus stove, and other small items. A few minutes later, the search was at an end. Some distance downslope, the doctor's body was found, almost completely buried in avalanche debris.

This sad find only confirmed the searchers' worst doubts, but all of them expressed considerable surprise that such a tragic event could take place on this insignificant-looking slope. The average angle was about 30–35°, although the starting zone, in a shallow gully, may have been slightly steeper. The thaw of the previous couple of days had altered the snow features somewhat, but the main dimensions of the avalanche were clearly visible. The *crownwall* at that time was no more than 30 cm high and only about 6 m wide. The victim was found about 50 m below this point, quite near the foot of the avalanche tip, which was approximately 17 m wide by 33 m long.

What can one learn from this unfortunate case? Clearly the hazards of solo winter mountaineering are again highlighted. More than that, the danger presented by local steepenings on otherwise fairly gentle slopes is brought out, along with the desirability of keeping to ridge crests in doubtful conditions. Perhaps the doctor had unintentionally diverged from his route or perhaps, like the rescue team, he thought the slope looked harmless; we will never know that, but if he made any error, its consequences were surely out of any proportion.

Carn Dearg Meadhonach, February 21, 1978

The mountain upon which this accident took place is part of the Carn Mor Dearg range in the Ben Nevis area and overlooks the Allt a'Mhuillin glen and Coire Leis. The following account is condensed from the excellent report prepared by Mr Terry Small, a member of the party concerned. He gives this description of the event:

"On Tuesday, February 21, 1978, a group of five climbers were descending the south-western slopes below Carn Dearg Mead-honach after completing the traverse of the Carn Mor Dearg Arête. They descended from the ridge on to the large easy-angled slopes; conditions were windless, with about one inch of fresh dry snow overlying a firm base for their crampons to dig in. There was no 'balling-up' of crampon points and conditions seemed excellent. The proliferation of rock islands and outcrops on the slope further added to their feeling of security. Forty-five minutes should have seen them to the CIC Hut, some 1,200 feet below at the foot of Coire Leis.

"The group stopped for a chocolate bar, naturally choosing a rocky island to rest on, in preference to the bare slope. The cloud cover began to break up at this point and fine views of Carn Dearg West and Coire na Ciste were obtained.

"Looking across to the south a broad ridge, liberally littered with rock debris, seemed to offer the natural way to the valley bottom, this route was chosen without discussion, it being one of those lines which experienced climbers would naturally choose.

"They left the rest stop and were traversing the slope, at this stage Jason Hunnisett was in the lead, followed by David Meadows, Terry Small, David Wilcoxson and George Jones, each spaced about ten yards apart. The positioning was purely random; no thought of danger was present. A shallow depression was being crossed, caused in part by the ridge for which the party was heading. The events of the next few seconds are not easy to remember in exact detail, but the concensus of the group is thus:

"A shock wave or motion of some sort made them look towards the top of the ridge some two hundred to two hundred and fifty feet above. At the same instant an explosive 'boom', exactly like gunfire coincided with a crack running across the slope one hundred feet above the party. The crack was extensive and was probably one hundred to one hundred and fifty feet wide and occurred above the whole of the party.

"Instantaneously the mass of snow below the break began to slide fairly slowly initially, downwards.

"David Meadows was caught on the edge of the moving slab, which was below the initial wide crack now confined to an area forty to sixty feet in width, but with quick reaction was able to run off on to firm ground.

"Terry Small, George Jones and David Wilcoxson ran north-westward, contouring the slope in an effort to outrun the crack extending above their heads in the same direction. After a few yards it seemed clear that the direction of flow was actually moving away from them; being channelled by the shallow depression one hundred feet below the break.

"They all turned to see Jason Hunnisett in the very centre of the accelerating slab, crouching as if regaining his balance and about to attempt to make for the side. At the same time the slab began to break up into large pieces some ten feet square around Jason and he was lost from sight as the whole mass disappeared into the mist below.

"Looking into the avalanche track as a way down, it showed areas of water ice pushing through the remaining snow layer, and so, after gathering their wits the party decided to descend the slope below them parallel with the avalanche path. In an attempt to minimise any further avalanche risk they quickly moved from rock to rock on their way down.

"Their feelings and state of mind at this stage can be imagined and their shouts for help whilst descending were heard by a member of the Pinnacle Club near the CIC Hut, she promptly radioed the Police, telling them that there had been an avalanche, and that she feared someone might have been injured.

"Some five to six hundred feet lower down the slope the texture of the snow showed a marked change, heavy 'balling-up' of crampons resulted in several slips which were arrested safely and the whole surface of the snow was covered with golf ball sized 'sun-balls' despite the absence of any sun on the slope that day. Some five hundred feet below this area and a total of approximately one thousand two hundred feet below the avalanche source, they came across the avalanche debris, and after searching they discovered the body of Jason Hunnisett, lying face upwards, head up the slope, some twenty inches below the snow surface. His knee protruding through the debris gave his position. His rucksack, straps torn from the rivets, lay nearby."

The fatal outcome of this accident is all the more tragic in view of the youth of the victim; cruelly ironic, too, when one learns that the party had abandoned plans to climb a gully and had chosen to traverse the Carn Mor Dearg arête "as an ultra-cautious alternative", when the temperature at the CIC hut had been seen to be above freezing.

According to Terry Small's notes, the two days prior to the accident had seen high winds blowing from the north-east, although Tuesday itself was windless. About 2 cm of new snow had fallen overnight, but most of the existing snow had fallen in severe, northerly gales three to four weeks before. Here we have a familiar pattern: new avalanche risk created by a change in wind direction. However, it would seem that the main, significant factor in the release of this avalanche was the exceptionally smooth nature of the bed surface. Large areas of blue ice are mentioned and in fact, the avalanche ran down the path of a frozen burn. The wind-slab lying on ice was an extremely dangerous situation, but would be impossible to identify without snowpit inspection and clearly the slope was of such an angle (25–30°) that few mountaineers would have considered this.

This accident may point out a need for us to be even more careful when cold weather has created ice in streambeds or open slopes, and to bear this in mind when making risk assessments later in the winter. To hear of incidents such as this can induce a type of fatalism. What can be the use of studying snow and avalanches if *any* slope can be dangerous? The alternative over-reaction of avalanche paranoia is equally unhelpful. We can only make our best judgments based on the knowledge we have gained and hope that our steps do not lead us into a hair-trigger situation such as that encountered by the luckless victim of this tragedy.

Ben Nevis, March 26, 1978

The northern cliffs of Ben Nevis and Carn Dearg are in every sense the crowning glory of the Scottish mountain scene. Few climbers can be unmoved by the sweeping slabs, and the great ridges buttressing the highest summit in the land. In winter, the magnificence of this scene is redoubled, with colourful hangings of green and blue ice decorating the crags. Little hint is given to the visitor on a fine winter's day of the menace that the cliffs can hold. On a normal day, however, with low cloud and spindrift swirling in the gullies the thoughts of the Ben Nevis climber might justifiably be more sombre. Many have remarked that the northern side of the Ben has an atmosphere only to be found elsewhere on the North Face of the Eiger. Significantly, the Ben has an Eiger-like story of tragedy and disaster: the occurrence of the unforeseeable is commonplace. Small wonder, then, that Ben Nevis has given birth to some of the most remarkable and destructive Scottish avalanches.

On March 26, 1978, there was a fair amount of activity on the Ben. A climber had been hurt in Observatory Gully and a RAF helicopter had been called to assist in the evacuation of the casualty. Late in the afternoon the helicopter was returning with the injured climber, passing the cliffs of Carn Dearg when the crew noticed some marks in the snow beneath the cliff. They appeared to be blood stains.

As the helicopter was coming down the Allt a'Mhuillin Glen, its progress had been observed by four young Irish hillwalkers. They were below the cliffs of Carn Dearg, some distance above the main path between Lochan Meall an-t-Suidhe and the CIC Hut, the main base for climbers on the Ben. They stopped to take photographs of the helicopter as it approached. By no stretch of the imagination were they in what could normally be called a dangerous position. But as the helicopter approached them, a mighty avalanche broke loose from the cliffs above and swept down towards them on a front of 250 m. No evasive or defensive action could be of any use in the face of such an overwhelming mass of snow. The tide broke over them and carried them down. Miraculously, as the avalanche came to a halt, three of the party were still on the surface, though partly buried and suffering from serious injuries. Of the fourth man, there was no trace.

This was one of the largest wet-snow avalanches ever seen in Scotland. We have said that this kind of avalanche is more easily foreseeable, and therefore, guarded against, than a wind-slab avalanche. But who would expect to be avalanched in such a place?

The injured walkers were quickly rescued and a search initiated for the missing man, although in truth the chances of a live rescue were small. Wet snow contains little air and can set round the victim like concrete, making breathing impossible. Despite the use of dogs, teams of probers and electronic equipment, the missing man was not found until the 28th. His body was located near the burn, some 100 m below the point where the avalanche struck him, perhaps the unluckiest of all the Ben's many victims.

Appendix 1

Use of Transceivers

Before starting out, the party must be practised in the use of transceivers and familiar with the particular set they are using. The sets must be equipped with batteries of the type recommended by the manufacturer and of good condition. Before departure the transmitting and receiving functions of each set must be checked, **the set switched on to "transmit" and worn securely under the clothing**. Sets that are switched off or that become detached provide no protection!

In the event of someone being lost in an avalanche, the rest of the party switch on to "search" (receive) and commence a long-range search. As soon as a signal is detected, the close-range search is used to pinpoint the victim.

Long-range Search

The aim is to cover the area of the debris so that a transceiver set to receive signals, passes well within the maximum transmission range of all points that a person might be buried. If the maximum range of the transmitter is about 30 m (a common value) suitable long-range search patterns would be:

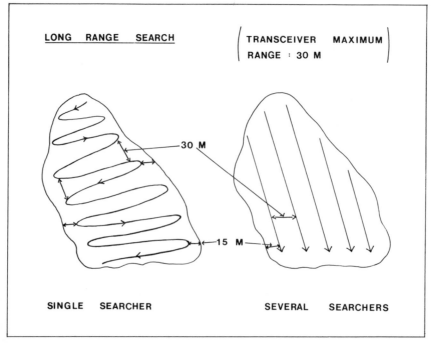

Figure 37

Close-range search

When a signal is detected (at A), rotate the receiver to get the best signal. Continue to walk in the original direction, until the signal begins to fade (at B). Return along the same line to the point where the maximum signal strength is obtained (C). Reduce the volume of the receiver to increase sensitivity and walk at right-angles to the first line. If the signal fades (at D), turn around and walk in the opposite direction. The signal should increase again. When it begins to fade again (at E) identify the maximum (at F), reduce the volume and repeat the process. One is now near the victim. The position is pinpointed when the transceiver is on minimum volume, and the signal fades if the receiver is moved in any direction.

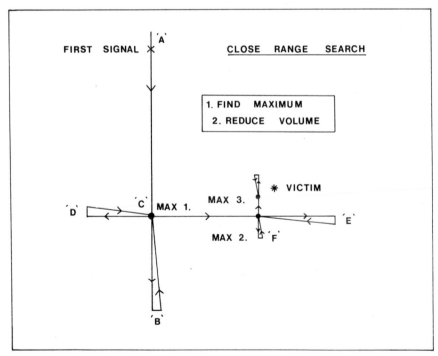

Figure 38

When searching for multiple victims, a normal long-range search pattern is used but when a signal is detected a single searcher follows this by close range searching, while the rest of the party continue the long-range search until the other signals have been detected.

If the victims are relatively close together multiple bleeps will be heard, and in this case, careful use of the volume control will usually allow the signals to be resolved and followed separately.

When the position has been pinpointed, the accuracy is about one third of the burial depth, so the search transceiver should be used from time to time to check that the hole is being dug in the optimum direction. It is at this stage that a collapsible shovel pays enormous dividends.

Finally, it should be noted that whilst searching, the rescuers are no longer protected by their own transceivers. Some sets such as Ortovox allow a rapid switching from "search" to "transmit" to reduce this hazard.

Appendix 2

Avalanche Classification

Several systems of avalanche classification exist. The mountaineer and skier do not require full scientific rigour; a simple five-point system is adequate.

Criterion

Type of release

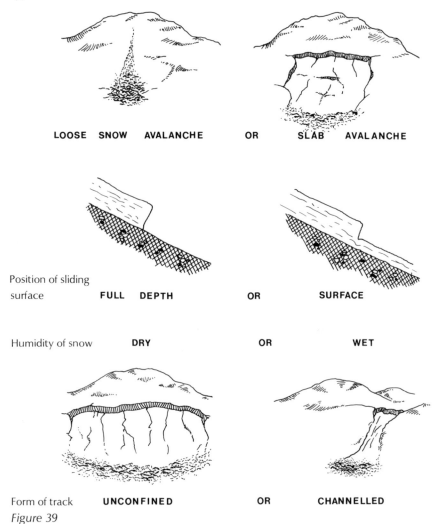

LOOSE SNOW AVALANCHE OR **SLAB AVALANCHE**

Position of sliding surface **FULL DEPTH** OR **SURFACE**

Humidity of snow **DRY** OR **WET**

Form of track **UNCONFINED** OR **CHANNELLED**

Figure 39

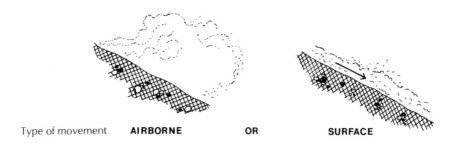

Type of movement   **AIRBORNE**   **OR**   **SURFACE**

Figure 39—continued

In rescue operations it is also of value to know the nature of the debris: i.e. Dry or Wet; Distinct Blocks or Mainly Homogenous; Contaminated or Uncontaminated (with rocks, earth).

Appendix 3

Avalanche Accident Black Spots

Despite the title, the sites noted in this appendix are not necessarily much more dangerous than other places, although for instance, the Castle Gullies area is known for its adverse rock stratification. Rather, or in addition, these black spots are notorious mainly because of their popularity. The provision of this list should not blind mountain-goers to the possibility that any slope may be a potential avalanche slope.

Climbing area	No. of accidents recorded	Comments
Raeburn's Gully, Lochnagar	5	Cornice and slope above main pitch have caused trouble
Trident Gullies (Cairngorm, Coire an t-Sneachda	4	Due to their common start, difficult to separate them
Great Slab (Cairngorm, Coire an Lochain)	4	Avoid like the plague in bad conditions
Castle Gullies, Ben Nevis	3	Traditional avalanche site
Coire Cas Headwall (Cairngorm)	3	Much traffic, many incidents, including very large avalanches
No 3 Gully (Ben Nevis)	3	Huge accumulations possible on all easy Ben gullies
No 5 Gully (Ben Nevis)	2	Site of some lucky escapes
Gardy Loo Gully (Ben Nevis)	2	
Garadh Gully (Ben Nevis)	2	
No 2 Gully (Ben Nevis)	2	

Climbing area	No. of accidents recorded	Comments
Great Gully (Buachaille Etive Mor)	2	
Coire Laogh Mor Headwall	2	NNE aspect particularly dangerous
Raeburn's Gully (Creag Meagaidh)	2	Meagaidh presents some wild avalanche terrain
Stob Coire nan Lochain (Glencoe)	4	Broad, Forked, Twisting Gullies and one unspecified location; one each at least

Appendix 4

Recommended Reading

The Avalanche Handbook, Perla and Martinelli, US Forest Service, 1976. Hard going but highly rewarding.
Avalanches and Snow Safety, Fraser (John Murray), 1966. (A revised edition of the *Avalanche Enigma*.) A very readable account of the avalanche problem in the Alps and the rescue work of the Davos Parsenndienst.
ABC of Avalanche Safety, La Chapelle (Cordee, Leicester, 1978). A concise handbook by a leading North American expert.
Mountaincraft and Leadership, Langmuir (Scottish Sports Council, 1984). Includes chapters on snow and avalanche. The author did much pioneer work on the subject in Scotland.
Avalanche, editors Harding *et al.* (Alpine Club, 1980). Proceedings of an Alpine Club Symposium with a number of useful case histories.
Avalanches Protection Location Rescue (Vanni Eigenmann Foundation, 1979). A detailed study of search and rescue techniques.
Avalanche Safety for Skiers and Climbers, Daffern (Diadem, 1983). A recent book with some coverage of Scotland and some good illustrations.
Snow Structures and Ski Fields, Seligman (London, 1936). The original classic of the field. Out of print and hard to obtain.

Appendix 5

Avalanche Accidents in Scotland: 1925 to Date

In period 1925–45, one or two accidents for which no details exist.

Key: (OS)—open slope avalanche; (B)—burial; (F)—fatality.

The following list is not exhaustive and there are undoubtedly errors. The authors would welcome comments, corrections, and additions so that the record may be as full as possible. Only accidents involving bodily injury or an MR call-out are listed. Doubtful cases and instances of collapsing ice-pitches are not included, but cornice collapses are. Undated incidents are not listed.

1938, November 27   Stob a'Coire Odhair, Blackmount (OS)
J. R. Wood (JMCS) and A. C. D. Small carried down 100–130 m by slab avalanche. Small injured but able to descend unaided.

1948, January 18   Sgurr Mor, Braemar (OS)
Four walkers carried down by avalanche. All injured and hospitalised.

1949, March 14   Ben Nevis (F)
Party of four (roped) St AUMC avalanched in No 5 Gully. Alison M. Bard (18) sustained concussion, died in hut.

1949   Lochnagar
Two roped parties carried down by cornice collapse in Raeburn's Gully. RAF team out.

1950, December 12   Ben Nevis
Rear Admiral Lauder (RN Ski and MC) avalanched in a gully; fractured leg.

1952, April 6   Cairngorm(F)
Crighton Allan (30), Edinburgh JMCS, avalanched in Coire an t-Sneachda—fatal. Other two members of party slightly injured. All JMCS—carried over Alladin Buttress—probably wind-slab.

1952, April 26   Cairngorm (2F)
John Harvey (30), Climber's Club, David Stead and Margoe Wearing avalanched in Coire an Lochain near top of climb. First two killed, third compound broken leg.

1953, April 1   Ben Nevis (2F) (2B)
Peter Drummond Smith (27) and David Munro (24), both experienced climbers, did not return to CIC hut after a climb. RAF and large local search parties out for six days. Bodies found April 19 roped together (rope unbroken) near foot of S Castle Gully. Presumed avalanched.

1957, February 23   Ben Lui (OS)
Avalanche near summit carried down four of Leuchars RAF Rescue Team. One broken leg. Blizzard conditions.

1959, March 8   Ben Nevis
Two naval ratings in No 2 Gully avalanched near top (new snow on old hard snow). Dislocated hip and chest injuries.

1960, January 30   Stob Coire nan Lochain
Dick Holt and Elizabeth Carruthers avalanched and fell to above Lochan. Girl had head injuries and broken jaw.

1960, February 14   Stob Coire nan Lochain
Two women (LSCC) climbing in Forked Gully, both avalanched. One had fractured spine and head injuries. Deep new snow.

1961, December 2   Aonach Eagach (F) (B)
Member of experienced party of three avalanched by powder snow just below Spot Height 3162. Avalanche area extended 230 m. Body found next day, completely buried.

1962, January 7   Buachaille Etive Mor (F)
Three climbers avalanched in Crowberry Gully, fell 300 m. One killed, two others injured. McInnes and Agnew avalanched 50 m on rescue.

1963, December 24   Ben Nevis
M. D. Taylor (17) and J. P. Charlesworth (25) avalanched; injuries. In Gardyloo Gully—fell 330 m into Observatory Gully. Wind-slab.

1964, December 28   Beinn a'Bhuird (2F) (OS) (3B)
Three members of party of four descending SW slopes towards Quoich Water involved in large avalanche and buried. One member not involved raised alarm. Two found dead, one alive after 22-hour burial.

1965, March 10   Coire an Lochain, Cairngorms (OS)
A hard slab avalanche 400 m in width, swept away three members of a party of eight descending to Lurcher's Meadow from the Plateau. Fell over 300 m and only saved by being so close to the actual line of fracture. Severe bruising.

1966, December 27   Coire Cas, Cairngorms (OS)
Party of two avalanched descending headwall of Coire Cas. Thick slab of snow broke off when halfway down. Partially buried—torn ligaments. Wind drifted snow accumulating previous week.

1967, January 27   Mam Sodhail (OS)
Peter Sheenan, instructor with party from Moray OB, descending ridge roping students down 45° snow slope. Snow avalanched 15–20 m either side of party. Leader pulled off ice-axe belay, fell about 30 m, hitting boulder—severe bruising head, chest, shoulders and scalp wound. Others uninjured.

1967, April 1   Ben Nevis (2B)
Two experienced climbers, D. Richardson and Philipson, in new snow avalanche in No 4 Gully. Carried 180 m on surface before both being buried. After nine hours Philipson freed himself, went to CIC. Rescue party found Richardson after ten hours, at midnight—had hand free. Exposure, slight frostbite.

1968, January 3   Cairngorm (OS) (2B)
Search party avalanched in Coire Raibert—Langmuir, Bathgate, Tiso, Briggs. Bathgate buried but dug out by others. Party retreated to Shelter Stone, Tiso and others evacuated by helicopter next morning—torn ligaments. Search party avalanched next day.

1968, February 6   An t-Sron (Glencoe) (OS)
RAF party of three thought to have taken wrong course descending in bad visibility. At 4.15 p.m. all carried down by wind-slab avalanche. Two escaped but Cpl McIver swept down much further; not badly injured.

1968, March 18   Ben Nevis
G. McNair (CUMC) carried down 100 m by cornice collapse. Rescued by helicopter.

1969, February 19   Cairngorm (OS)
Nine members of Glenmore Lodge Winter Survival Course avalanched on W side of Coire Cas at 11.30 a.m. Help from other parties and Ski Patrol. All casualties at Shieling by 12.45 p.m. Six hospitalised, two serious.

1970, January 18   Ben Nevis (3F) (3B)
Four very experienced climbers avalanched near top of Italian Climb. One not attached to rope at time survived. Others found dead in debris at foot of climb. Slab avalanche.

1970, February 7   Buachaille Etive Mor (3B) (F)
Gunn Clark (34), very experienced, and three others avalanched by wet snow in Great Gully, carried about 70 m. Clark and two others buried, others dug out but Clark could not be found at once—buried 1–2 m deep, unconscious when found—could not be revived.

1970, February 16   Ciste Dubh (OS) (B)
Party of five St AUMC climbing SE shoulder. At about 900 m, new snow on snow ice. At 4 p.m., whole party avalanched 100 m. Three dug themselves out and after five minutes found fourth (finger sticking out of snow) unconscious with head injury. Others—one broken ankle, one head wound.

1972, February 12   Glen Clova
Two Dundee University students avalanched in B Gully, Corrie Fee; thaw conditions. Fractured femur and arm and facial injuries.

1972, February 12   Aonach Dubh a'Ghlinne (Glencoe) (OS)
EUMC party carried 180 m in new snow avalanche. Snow had fallen 24 hours previously. Minor injuries caused by ice-axe (GR 118548).

1972, February 13   Lochnagar
Girl leading Raeburn's Gully knocked off by small powder avalanche; broken leg.

1972, April 16   Lochnagar
Party of three avalanched by cornice in Raeburn's Gully. One badly gashed leg.

1973, December 1   Ben Nevis
Heriot Watt UMC party of three set out to climb No 3 Gully. Fine, cold. Carried 180 m by slab avalanche; one stretcher case, broken arm. Others, bruising and cuts.

1973, December 19   Cairngorm
Glenmore Lodge instructor Peter Boardman carried 180 m by avalanche in Alladin's Couloir, Coire an t-Sneachda. Injured knee.

1973, December 23   Cairngorm
Two young English climbers carried 100 m by avalanche in Coire an t-Sneachda; slight injuries, evacuated by helicopter.

1974, March 17   Cairngorm (OS)
Two Irish climbing instructors carried away by soft slab avalanche. One abdominal injury, one broken tib. and fib. Coire Laogh Mor.

1974, April 7   Cairngorm
Two climbers carried down by cornice avalanche in Coire an Lochain. One minor head injury, one broken ankle.

1975, January 19   Ben Nevis
Party of two on Hadrian's Wall. Leader avalanched and slightly hurt. Rescued next morning.

1975, January 19   Ben Nevis
English climber avalanched in Tower Gully—broken ribs and ankle.

1975, January 19   Beinn Achaladair (OS)
Three young climbers (Lomond MC) climbing steep slope unroped, avalanched; all fell 180 m. Two stretcher cases—one broken femur, one broken ribs and lacerations, one puncture wound by ice-axe.

1975, January 19   Stob Coire nan Lochain
Party of two (SMC and Rannoch Club) descending Broad Gully when minor avalanche started. Carried them down—one fractured ankle, one suspected rib injury.

1975, March 30   Cairngorm (OS)
Two RAF climbers traversing top of Great Slab, Coire an Lochain, when large slab avalanche broke away. Ankle and knee injuries.

1975, March 30   Lairig Ghru (OS)
Eight members of Scottish Ski Club on ski tour avalanched on N side of Lairig near Sinclair Hut. Three injured—evacuated by helicopter. Sudden temperature rise.

1976, February 14   Cairngorm (F)
Young Scottish climber knocked from steps by small avalanche at foot of Red Gully, Coire an t-Sneachda. Unable to brake with axe and hit boulders. Died in hospital.

1976, March 12   Cairngorm (OS)
Glenmore Lodge party avalanched on Goat Track, Coire an t-Sneachda. Broken leg and other injuries.

1976, March 12   Cairngorm (OS) (F)
Other Glenmore Lodge party on way to assist at above incident avalanched in Coire an Lochain near col on Fiacaill a'Coire an t-Sneachda. Six injured, one died in hospital.

A Chance in a Million

1976, March 13   Cairngorm (F)
Experienced English climber avalanched at top of Runnel, Coire an t-Sneachda.
Fell 50 m. Held by second but killed.

1976, March 14   Lochnagar
Two Inverness climbers in Raeburn's Gully, unroped. One hit by small avalanche
and fell to foot of climb; broken femur.

1976, March 14   Bidean nam Bian
Scottish climber descending Central Gully when caught in wet snow avalanche
and swept 230 m, passing over 10 m rock face and ending in coire basin below.
Fractured femur, fractured clavicle and ribs.

1977, February 3   Ben Nevis (F) (B)
Two climbers in cornice avalanche in South Castle Gully, fell 270 m. One severely
injured right arm, other buried 2 m deep and found dead.

1977, February 15   Ben Nevis (F) (B)
Two English climbers climbing in area of Garadh Gully when one decided to return
due to exhaustion. Companion completed climb, returned to CIC; no trace of
companion. Finally found dead buried 2 m deep in avalanche.

1977, March 23   Cairngorm
Don Roscoe (UCNW) avalanched in Central Gully, Coire an t-Sneachda, to about
30 m above Lochan; broken lower left leg.

1977, March 29   Ben Nevis (OS)
Two Middlesex climbers avalanched in Coire Eoghainn; one head injury, one
leg injury.

1977, April 20   Ben Nevis (F)
Two climbers having completed ascent of Point Five were stood 3 m and 5 m
respectively from cornice edge. Cornice collapsed carrying down man at 3 m
distance.

1977, December 28   Cairngorm (OS)
Two climbers avalanched beneath The Vent, Coire an Lochain; one injured leg.

1978, January 21   Cairngorm
A. J. Davies (20) and I. James (22) avalanched at foot of cliffs in Coire an t-
Sneachda. Head injuries and broken knee.

1978, January 21   Cairngorm
B. J. Clough (19, English) and R. Wells (18, Scottish) avalanched in Coire an t-
Sneachda, believed in Central Gully. First had head and pelvis injuries, second
exposure.

1978, January 21   Lochnagar (F)
I. Greenhill (22) St AUMC and S. Crosier (19) swept 230 m by slab avalanche in
Raeburn's Gully. Greenhill killed, Crosier rescued alive.

1978, February 19   Cairngorm (OS)
Party of hillwalkers avalanched in Coire Laogh Mor by slab 400 m across. One
injured—assistance from Cairngorm Ski Patrol.

1978, February 21   Carn Mor Dearg (OS) (B) (F)
Climbing instructor Jason Hunnisett (19) carried 400 m by large wind-slab avalanche. Buried and though dug out quickly could not be revived.

1978, March 26   Ben Nevis (B) (F)
Four Irish students caught in huge wet snow avalanche on path from CIC hut to Lochan Meall an t-Suidhe. Three injured (one fractured skull); one buried and found dead on 28th.

1978, December 19   Cairngorm (OS)
Five persons carried away by 1 m thick slab avalanche on Great Slab, Coire an Lochain. Two injured.

1978, December 26   Braeriach (OS) (2B) (2F)
Two walkers, Ian Kershaw and Colin Shaw, missing on Braeriach on 25th. Bodies found buried in large avalanche in Coire Bogha-Cloiche.

1979, February 23   Cairngorm (OS)
Climber avalanched below Fiacaill Couloir and carried down about 70–100 m. Cracked pelvis and lower leg. Slab about 100 m across, 15–50 cm thick.

1979, February 28   Ben Nevis
Six men swept down No 5 Gully by cornice which collapsed as it was being tunnelled. Most fell 100 m unhurt, but M. Pearce sustained ice-axe injury in groin.

1979, April 8   Ben Nevis (B) (F)
Two climbers, H. Welsh and C. Fraser, approaching foot of Italian Climb, swept away by small slab avalanche falling from above into Garadh Gully. Welsh buried, Fraser escaped. Welsh found dead, buried 1 m deep near foot of avalanche tip, after 15 minutes searching. Asphyxia. Weather conditions "Good but mild," and 1°C, snow flurries, soft dry snowfall 24 hours earlier.

1980, January 20   Lochnagar (B)
Two climbers in powder avalanche below Parallel Gully A. One injured (collapsed lung; broken rib) but rescued by other climber. Other found alive by rescuers after $8\frac{1}{2}$ hours burial—fingers of both hands showing. Unconscious; hypothermic; femur fracture; frostbite. Carried 130 m by avalanche.

1980, February 21   Ben Nevis
Party of two decided to climb No 3 Gully Buttress as gullies were liable to avalanche (weather good but mild). Both swept from top of first pitch by small avalanche. Man (28) cracked a leg bone. Other uninjured went for help. Lochaber MRT; RAF helicopter.

1980, November (ND)   Cairngorm (OS)
Experienced Edinburgh climber avalanched at foot of Hell's Lum Crag. Injury to hip joint.

1980, March 5   Glencoe
Foot of Twisting Gully of Stob Coire an Lochain. Two men (43 and 25) caught in a powder-snow avalanche funnelled due to hour-glass configuration. Light snowfall previous night. One with head and shoulder injuries, one uninjured. RAF helicopter.

1980, March 16   Cairngorm (OS)
Two climbers in soft slab avalanche beneath Aladdin's Buttress, Coire an t-Sneachda. One hurt, evacuated by other climbers. Debris about 20 m wide.

1980, March 17   Creag Meagaidh
Raeburn's Gully. Party of seven or eight climbing gully. Small slab avalanche took three down, but two stopped after 6 m. Man (37) fell 170 m. Broken pelvis and ribs. Lochaber MRT, RAF helicopter, 45 man-hours.

1980, March 17   An Garbhanach
Three men about to traverse below cornice when it collapsed, carrying them down 150 m. Brought down to Steall, but stretchered out from there. Severe bruising and broken ribs.

1980, March 18   Ben Nevis
Three climbers avalanched, two hurt, evacuated by Lochaber MRT.

1981, February 11   Creag Meagaidh
Six from Plas-y-Brenin party avalanched in Cinderella Gully, slab avalanche. Two instructors sustained broken legs, two others hurt.

1981, February 21   Lochnagar; Parallel Gully A
Three Scottish climbers in slab avalanche. One hurt (fell 90 m). Ribs, chest, leg injuries. Rescued by other climbers and AMRT. Evacuation in darkness by helicopter.

1981, February 21   Glencoe
Two English climbers avalanched into Central Gully, Stob Coire nam Beith. One slightly injured, other head injuries.

1981, October 28   Ben Nevis
Five people avalanched in area of No 3 Gully, carried 300 m. One girl fractured wrist and injured ribs. English party.

1982, January 5   Ben Nevis (OS)
Heavy snow and blowing (also night before). Two climbers below Point Five Gully. One avalanched—OK, other left above crown surface fracture—had to be helicoptered off. Reported to be 2 m wall. Debris reached over Allt a'Mhuilinn at foot of Observatory Gully.

1982, January 14 or 15   Beinn a'Ghlo (B) (F) (OS)
Experienced hillwalker on solo walking expedition missing for five days. Body found on 20th, buried in slab avalanche on NW side of Beinn a'Ghlo, only hand protruding.

1982, January 18   Bidean nan Bian —(B)
Two policemen (20 and 24) climbing in Lost Valley, carried down by large avalanche. One badly bruised, other buried up to chest but dug out by companion after half an hour. Glencoe team called out by party member not caught.

1982, February 15   Ben Nevis (2B) (2F)
Five English climbers avalanched in Castle Gullies area. Two found dead and another seriously injured.

1982, February 15   Ben Nevis (F)
Four English climbers avalanched in Gardyloo Gully. One girl dead, one man—
fractured femur.

1982, February 15   Ben Nevis
Unidentified climber injured in avalanche in No 2 Gully. Two broken arms, but
walked down. Then airlifted by helicopter.

1982, February 15   Creag Meagaidh
Three climbers from outdoor centre avalanched in Raeburn's Gully. One man
broke leg in 170 m fall, others uninjured.

1982, March 8   Buachaille Etive Mor (OS)
Three climbers traversing snow slope to descend Curved Ridge, when two were
avalanched for 80 m. Glencoe Mountain Rescue Team out.

1982, March 17   Ben Nevis
Two climbers descending to Carn Mór Dearg Arête when cornice fractured 5 m
back from edge. One fell short way; other fell 300 m. Broken ribs and internal
injuries.

1982, December 27   Ben Nevis
Four men avalanched 130 m from near top of No 3 Gully. One injured (spiked
through the knee by crampon) and stretchered down. Others had cuts and
bruises. Wind-slab avalanche. There had been no wind-slab at foot of gully.
Generally good snow conditions.

1983   Ben Nevis
Climber (male 21) 13 m from top of Bob Run. Fell 230 m when slab gave way. Seen
by RAF Kinloss MRT. Chest and facial bruises. No fractures.

1983, January 29   Cairngorms
Large area of ice veneer came away from underlying snow. Ankle injury to one
member of Tayside MRT on exercise (male 36). 30 m fall arrested by axe braking
and grabbing handrail. Easy Gully of Winter Corrie, Dreish.

1983, February 17   Cairngorms
Party of four ascending Pinnacle Gully. Man (34) caught in wind-slab avalanche
and fell 330 m, tearing knee ligaments. Northern Constabularly—4 man-hours.